THE UPSTART GUIDE TO

OWNING AND MANAGING A CONSULTING SERVICE

THE UPSTART GUIDE TO
OWNING AND MANAGING A CONSULTING SERVICE

Dan Ramsey

UPSTART PUBLISHING
Specializing in Small Business Publishing
a division of Dearborn Publishing Group, Inc.

*Have two goals: wisdom—that is, knowing and doing
right—and common sense. Don't let them slip away, for
they fill you with living energy, and bring you honor and
respect.*

—Proverbs 3:21-22

Executive Editor: Bobbye Middendorf
Managing Editor: Jack Kiburz
Cover Design: Paul Perlow Design

© 1995 by Dan Ramsey

Published by Upstart Publishing Company, Inc.,
a division of Dearborn Publishing Group, Inc.

Printed in the United States of America

95 96 97 10 9 8 7 6 5 4 3 2 1
Library of Congress Cataloging-in-Publication Data
Ramsay, Dan, 1945–
        The upstart guide to owning and managing a consulting service / by
Dan Ramsey.
        p.   cm.
    Includes index.
    ISBN 0-936894-81-4
        1. Consulting firms—Management—Handbooks, manuals, etc.
2. Business consultants—Handbooks, manuals, etc. 3. New business
enterprises—Management—Handbooks, manuals, etc. I. Title.
HD69-C6R37   1995   95-6615
001'.068—dc20   CIP

CONTENTS

PREFACE AND ACKNOWLEDGMENTS

Consulting is a $17-billion-a-year business! As a consultant you will provide professional advice or service to businesses and consumers. You don't have to be an expert in your field, but you must know where to find practical answer. You must be inquisitive and resourceful, a helpful listener, and a problem solver.

In business, it's not what you know that makes you succeed but what you don't know that reduces your chances of success. So success comes from discovering what you don't know about your chosen business opportunity and learning it. Maybe it's a lack of management experience, or marketing skills, or financial background, or technical knowledge, or money.

The Upstart Guide to Owning and Managing a Consulting Service will guide you through the steps of selecting a field of knowledge, developing that knowledge, and finding clients who will pay you well for your advice. It includes detailed examples from successful business and consumer consultants. Business and trade terms are defined in context. Specific resources with addresses and phone numbers are included. Each chapter ends with "Action Guidelines," a list of actions you can take to reach your business goals.

Also included are worksheets, forms, and examples to help you increase profits while reducing risks. This guide clearly explains the opportunities and pitfalls of consulting for business and consumers, and includes specific pricing recommendations for a variety of consulting services. It shows you how to write proposals and contracts that clearly confirm the scope of your work and the payment you'll receive.

The Upstart Guide to Owning and Managing a Consulting Service is your guide to success with your own small business. As the author of more than 50 business and consumer books—and a business consultant myself—I will guide you through the proven steps to starting and operating your own consulting service. I will show you how to set your prices, build your business, pay your taxes, and enjoy what you do.

If you're a marketing consultant, the chapter on marketing will be a review. The same will be true of other chapters for business consultants. However, you'll find chapters on start-up, financing, day-to-day operations, and growing your business to guide you in owning and managing your consulting service.

A successful consulting service can be helpful to others and profitable to you. This book will help you do both.

Acknowledgments

Thanks to many people who contributed to the development of this book. They include Hal Wright of The Wright Track; Claire Rosenzweig of the Institute of Management Consultants; Bill Stinehart, Vito Tanzi, and James Bickmann of the American Association of Professional Consultants; Donna-Jean Rainville of The Consulting Source, Inc.; Herman Holtz, consulting guru; Spencer Smith, Karen Billipp and Jean Kerr of Upstart Publishing; David H. Bangs, Jr., author of *The Business Planning Guide;* Lori Capps and Roy L. Fietz of the Business Development Center at Southwest Oregon Community College; and The Small Business Administration Office of Business Development. Thanks also to the staffs of Ramsey Business Strategies and Communication Solutions for assisting with the production of this book.

Business forms in this book were produced using Per-FORM Forms Designer from Delrina Technology Inc. and Key Draw! Plus from SoftKey Software Products Inc.

OPPORTUNITIES FOR CONSULTING SERVICES

I t is said that a consultant is anyone who carries a briefcase and comes from more than 200 miles away. That's not quite true, but it reflects the icon that a consultant is someone with objective knowledge.

Actually, a *consultant* is someone who sells advice to those who want it. Useful advice may be developed through the consultant's knowledge of a subject, the skill of problem solving, or the ability to research.

Consulting is very big business. There are currently more than 80,000 consultants in the United States serving a wide variety of clients. They range in size from Andersen Consulting in Chicago with annual revenues nearing $3 billion to a part-time image consultant earning $25,000 a year.

The purpose of this first chapter is to acquaint you with the business of selling advice. You'll be introduced to a typical consulting service, learn what business and consumer consultants do, view a representative business day for a consultant, look at what consultants sell and how they sell it, and select your field of consulting. You'll then see how this decision will impact your life and your earnings. Finally, this chapter will give you specific steps you can take to putting what you've learned into action.

Meet Pioneer Communications, Inc.

Pioneer Communications is a business communications consulting service in the Pacific Northwest. President Walter Curtis had 15 years of experience in the marketing communications field before striking out on his own. Actually, he was pushed.

As project manager for a training service, Walt was responsible for producing industrial training manuals in the pulp and paper industry. He had risen from writer to project coordinator, to project manager. After four years, the training contract ended and none took its place. Walt was out of a job. He had previously worked as a copywriter for a large regional advertising agency. Before that he had been a staff writer for a business publication. Walt knew business and he knew communications. He just didn't know what he was going to do next.

Fortunately, he heard about a small writing project through a trade association of which he was a member. The project would only last four weeks, they said, but would pay about twice what Walt previously made in a month. He took it. The small project grew into a larger project, as they sometimes do. Fortunately, Walt's agreement required a per diem (per day) rather than a flat fee for the project. The longer the project lasted, the more Walt was paid.

Three months later, Walt decide that he couldn't count on an eternal project so he took a day off to pursue other contracts. Walt came up with a business name that sounded like he had been a communications consultant longer than anyone else— Pioneer Communications—and had business cards made up. He wrote a short brochure listing his experience and qualifications. He set up four appointments for the day and started making the rounds. He soon had sufficient jobs to carry him for the next eight months. Walt was in business for himself.

Today, Pioneer Communications consults with high-tech businesses in the Willamette Valley. It helps them define their communication goals, find writers and other resources, and reviews their marketing documents to make sure they are efficient. Pioneer Communications charges $125 an hour for consulting services with a 10 percent discount for prepayment. Writing projects are bid at $80 an hour. Walt has one full-time and one part-time associate that help him develop communication projects. Both work as independent contractors on a percentage.

After two difficult years, Walt has sufficient contracts to begin taking Friday afternoons off. He justifies it by saying, "I'm the boss!"

What a Business Consultant Does

There are two general fields of consultants: those who advise businesses and those who help consumers. The next two topics will explain the differences and suggest subjects in each category that may fit your qualifications and interests.

The purpose of business is to make a profit. That's true of your business as well as all other businesses. If you have training or experience in general or specific aspects of business, consider building a consulting service on that foundation.

There are dozens of other fields. Business consultants earn $50 to $150 and more per hour. Some travel extensively. Others work exclusively from their home using the telephone and fax.

National general management firms such as McKinsey and Company, and major accounting firms with consulting divisions such as Coopers & Lybrand, have consultants that specialize by function, industry, or region. Smaller consulting firms also frequently specialize in subcategories of a field, such

Businesses need advice and help with:

- Accounting
- Acquisitions
- Advertising
- Banking
- Communications
- Construction
- Data Processing
- Medical and
  Dental Services
- Economics
- Education
- Engineering
- Entrepreneurship
- Executive Search
- Finance
- Health Care
- Hotel/Restaurant
  Operation
- Import/Export
- Insurance
- International Business
- Investments
- Management
- Marketing
- Municipal Government
- Packaging
- Pension
- Personnel
- Printing and Graphics
- Production
- Public Relations
- Publishing
- Purchasing
- Quality Control
- Real Estate
- Records Management
- Recreation
- Research and
  Development
- Retail Sales
- Scientific
- Telecommunications
- Traffic and
  Transportation
- Training
- Travel

as consulting on investments in real estate or offering advice on finding and applying for research grants in the chemical industry. In many cases, the more specialized the knowledge, the higher the fees.

One consulting service may decide to advise personnel departments in paper mills. Another may choose to serve all businesses within a geographic region with annual sales of $1 million to $5 million. A third consulting service may advise pension plan administrators on taxation. Still another may offer aerospace engineering services to foreign manufacturers.

In addition, a consulting service may decide to specialize in one of two approaches to advising clients. The service may emphasize the resolution of an issue or the transfer of needed skills to the client. For example, a restaurant with cash flow problems may only need advice on how to resolve that specific problem. Or the owner may need to be trained in advanced cash flow forecasting and other aspects of business management.

There are advantages and disadvantages to both approaches for the consultant and the client. Problem resolution is less expensive for the client, but may not solve the underlying cause. Skill transfer is more expensive for the client, but reduces dependency on the consultant.

What a Consumer Consultant Does

Businesses aren't the only clients for useful advice. Consumers also need informed help making decisions.

Consult with consumers on one of a variety of topics:
- Astrology
- Beauty and Fashion
- Career Planning
- Cooking
- Dealing With Death
- Defensive Driving
- Estate Planning
- Health Issues

- Home Decorating
- Job Hunting
- Memory Development
- Organization
- Party Planning
- Personal Shopping
- Pet Selection and Care
- Retirement Planning
- Shyness
- Time Management
- Wardrobe Selection
- Wedding Planning
- Writing

These are just a few of the hundreds of subjects. Consumer consultants typically earn $35 to $90 an hour. Some consumer consultants work in a retail location with gross sales of $1 million a year or more. Others operate part-time from their homes, bringing in $10,000 to $50,000 a year of income.

Within these fields, there are many areas of specialization that can be selected to fit your client's needs as well as your own interests and skills. For example, you may decide to specialize in advising clients how to select an animal shelter pet that has the appropriate personality and temperament for their needs. Or you may specialize in helping college students manage their time more efficiently. Or you may have qualifications to offer advice on planning an Islamic wedding ceremony.

Consumer consultants typically aren't paid as much as business consultants. The primary reason is that a business can financially benefit from useful advice, and so is in a position to pay more for that advice. In addition, credentials for a business consultant are often more difficult and expensive to obtain that those for a consumer consultant. Even so, a consumer consultant with strong credentials and valuable advice serving a specific market can make an excellent income.

Typical Business Day for a Consultant

There are no typical consultants so there are really no typical days for a consultant. That's what makes it fun. One successful investment consultant in California works during New York Stock Exchange hours, quitting about 2 P.M. Pacific time each afternoon. She is then ready to greet her three children as they come in from school. An export consultant who specializes in Pacific Rim countries works late at night when Japanese, Korean, Chinese, and Taiwanese businesses are open. A successful home decorating consultant prefers to work weekends only.

Most important to a consultant is time. Getting the most value from each moment is important, especially when someone is paying you for those moments. Depending on the type of consulting done, appointment schedules may be kept and closely followed. Besides tools of the trade, the two most important tools for most consultants are an appointment calendar and a priority list. A successful consultant in nearly any trade will refer to these tools many times a day.

The Market for Consulting Services

Chapter 6 will extensively cover the many ways you can market your business or consumer consulting service. For now, let's look at marketing in general and help you see that marketing is both vital and fun.

The purpose of marketing is simply to bring product and client together. To do this, you will first determine who your client is. For example, the client of a printing consultant is any business that uses printing services: larger businesses that produce documents, literature, forms, or packaging materials. If the specialization is packaging, clients are manufacturers who must package their product for the consumer.

By first defining your client you can then define your market. For example, as a printed packaging consultant with industry contacts in the Chicago area you can easily define your market and even buy lists of all prospects who may use your service.

Defining your market for a consumer consulting service is somewhat different. If you plan to advise people on selecting appropriate pets from an animal shelter, you will define two markets:

- People who consider the animal shelter as a source of pets but don't know how to make the best selection
- People who have not previously considered an animal shelter as a source of good pets

Once defined, your potential clients can be reached in a variety of ways. Again, Chapter 6 will help you define and reach the appropriate markets for your consulting service.

Consulting in the Information Age

Technology has impacted all aspects of modern life for both businesses and consumers. Technology offers many tools to help consultants become and stay informed as well as to help their clients.

For example, a successful direct-marketing consultant serves clients throughout the United States without ever leaving her rural home in South Dakota. Her office is in her house, has three incoming telephone lines for voice and faxes, has an answering system that sounds like she has a receptionist, and has a computer system for quickly developing graphic layouts for clients. From her office she can simultaneously send her monthly client newsletter by fax to over 100 locations. She sends and receives dozens of electronic mail messages from clients and resources each day. She even does her banking by computer modem. She will soon install an inexpensive video telephone conferencing system for face-to-face meetings with her primary clients in New York City and in Los Angeles.

A consumer consultant specializing in cooking can use electronic bulletin boards to send and receive recipes, plan menus, and communicate with other cooking consultants. Specialized computer programs help plan menus based on dietary needs and serving requirements.

In Chapter 2 you'll learn about the tools of technology that successful consultants use and how to select them.

Primary Consulting Services

As with all businesses, consultants perform a *process*. A process is a series of operations required in making a product or furnishing a service. The process of making a hamburger, for example, requires knowledge (how to prepare), materials (meat, bun, pickle, special sauce), labor (cooking, assembling, packaging), and results in a specific output (a hamburger) in a form that the client wants.

There is a process to producing consulting services. Understanding the mechanics of the process—the required knowledge, materials, labor, and expected results—will make you a better and more efficient consultant.

Consultants who solve specific problems for clients typically follow a four-step process:

1. Diagnose

2. Design

3. Implement

4. Measure

For example, a marketing consultant would diagnose the client's situation and its cause, design a marketing campaign to solve the problem, implement or help the client implement the campaign, then measure the results to determine whether the expected results were achieved. The diagnosis may determine that sales are down because business has been lost to a competitor on pricing. In this case, the marketing consultant designs a campaign that stresses value over price, then implements the campaign by developing ads and sales literature. Finally, the consultant determines if sales to the target market—clients that had moved to competitors—have increased.

The process for your consulting may be different, depending on what services you offer, to whom you offer them, what results are expected, and whether you solve problems for them or tranfer skills to them.

The knowledge required for producing consulting services includes oral and written communication skills, fundamentals of business, and extensive knowledge within your specialty. Your consulting service will also be more efficient if you understand business management and the use of computers and software. Chapter 3 will offer numerous resources for developing your knowledge and skills.

The materials you will need for consulting services are basic: office equipment and supplies, communication tools, reference materials, marketing materials, and any specialized tools or equipment.

Of course, your consulting service will require labor. In fact, most consulting services are labor-intensive. That is, most of what the client is paying for is your time rather than a physical product. You may perform all the labor yourself or get help from employees, independent contractors, subcontractors, associates, or other outside services. In each case, you must understand what the labor requirements of the process are to ensure that the job is being done properly and efficiently.

Finally, you need to define the end result you want. Actually, it is not the final step; it is the first one. Until you understand exactly what your client requires, you cannot define the other elements in your process: knowledge, materials, and labor.

For example, you must decide that the client's need is to increase sales or have a successful event or reduce employee problems before you can develop the specific steps to reach the client's goal. You cannot efficiently define the components of your process until you have defined your output. In our earlier example, you don't select beef as a material until you've decided that a hamburger is the output or end result you want. You can't make hamburgers using tofu.

All this may sound quite elementary. It is. But it is where more new businesses get lost than anywhere else. They start out with the wrong knowledge, materials, and labor for their clients' needs. They look at their solution before they've even discovered what a client's problem is. They start at the wrong end of the process. This book will guide you in discovering and developing the best—and most profitable—process for your consulting service.

Other Products and Services Consultants Provide

Depending on what type of consulting you do, there may be other products and services you can provide to increase your market as well as your income.

For example, a construction consultant may offer a subscription newsletter, books, reports, and other documents to prospects and clients. In addition, the consultant may speak on related topics for a fee or at no charge to promote the business. Doing so makes the consultant an expert. It also brings the consultant into contact with potential clients.

Consider what other products and services you could offer for various consulting ventures. An image consultant can produce and sell videos on how to enhance beauty and image. A quality control consultant can write an important book on that subject for a specific industry. A job-hunting consultant can also advise employers on how to hire effective people.

Selecting Your Field

By now, you may have a number of ideas for consulting services you could offer. Remember, they don't have to be only areas in which you are an expert. They can also be areas in which you would like to become an expert and are willing to train yourself.

To develop a list of potential fields of consulting, ask yourself:

- What training have I completed?
- What business experience have I had?
- What are my interests and hobbies?
- What skills and attributes do I have?
- What do I enjoy doing for others?
- Do I prefer working with people directly or indirectly?
- What knowledge and skills will I need to become an effective consultant?

The topic of assessing your personal goals, covered in Chapter 2, will offer additional focusing questions to help you decide both what you want to do and how you want to do it.

How to Find the Tools You'll Need

Once you've selected your field of consulting, deciding what tools you will need will be relatively easy. For example, someone who sells good advice on retail sales will not only need experience in this field, but also need to know what the latest statistics, tools, and trends are. For this, the retail sales consultant will have numerous contacts within the field, subscribe to a variety of publications, gather and study books on retail sales and related topics, and develop experience and credentials in solving retail sales problems.

Chapter 3 offers resources for consultants including professional associations, trade journals, and books. Of course, the resouces for your specific field may not be included as there are hundreds of specialized topics on which consultants advise. A comprehensive listing of trade and consumer associations is available at most public libraries under the title *Encyclopedia of Associations* (Gale Research, 1994).

Your Life as a Consultant

What can you expect your life to be like if you decide to become a professional consultant? That depends. If you're a square peg trying to fit into a round hole, you will be uncomfortable. If you don't enjoy solving problems and using your skills to help people, you will probably be miserable. If you're looking for a way to get rich quick, try another line of work—one I haven't discovered yet. But if you enjoy helping other people, you have good communication skills or a strong desire to develop them, experience and/or training in your field, and the need to be an independent businessperson, offering consulting services may be a rewarding way of making a living.

In addition, operating a successful consulting service can help you develop the lifestyle you desire. If you enjoy traveling, consulting can pay you for doing it. If you'd prefer to work from home, consulting can fund a home office. If you enjoy meeting new people, consulting can make you both well known and popular.

Most important, a well-managed consulting service can help you find financial security and a sense of significance that few other professions offer.

How Much You Can Earn as a Consultant

How much can you expect to make operating a consulting business? Of course, that depends on local need, competition, your skills, and other factors. But there are some guidelines that will get you started.

First, the typical consulting service operated by the owner without employees can sell about $70,000 to $100,000 in services in a year. That's earning a rate of $70 to $100 an hour, four hours a day, five days a week. The other four-plus hours a day will be spent on marketing and administration duties. Few consulting services start out the first year making that much, but most can do so by the second full year of operation.

How much profit should you expect to make? As a service business, much of your income will go to pay for labor (Figure 1.1, on page 15). In a one-person office, that's you. During the second year of operation, your salary will be approximately 40 percent of income. That's $28,000 to $40,000 in salary for our example. Overhead expenses (rent, telephone, advertising, equipment) will take about 25 percent of your income. Direct expenses (letterheads, envelopes, books, subscriptions, etc.) will typically take ten percent of your income. What's left over is profit: about 25 percent of income. Taxes come from this figure before you can call it net profit.

The above figures are for your second year of operation when you've developed repeat and referral business, have developed a target market, and purchased your equipment and supplies. Your first year will be more difficult as you build your business. During the first year, expect about 75 percent of your estimated income and overhead to be as high as 40 percent of income. That is, if you estimate that second-year sales will total $72,000, estimate first-year sales to be 75 percent of that, or about $54,000. Your salary will be about $21,600 (40 percent), overhead will be higher at approximately $21,600 (40 percent), direct expenses of about $5,400 (10 percent), and

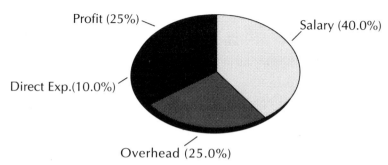

Figure 1.1: Typical expenses and profit percentages for second year of operation of a consulting service.

profit before taxes of about $5,400 (10 percent) or about $0 after taxes. Don't plan on getting rich the first year and you won't be disappointed.

The above numbers are averages. In fact, a business consultant may only bill 25 percent of available hours and a consumer consultant with both products and services to sell may be profitable after three months.

Should you add an employee? Only if you are certain that you will increase income by at least *three times* the employee's salary. For example, to hire an employee at $20,000 a year (about $10 an hour), make sure the employee's services will bring you at least $60,000 in business during the coming year. That's a minimum. Some service businesses use multipliers of four or even five to determine whether they can afford to hire additional staff. Remember that about 40 percent of your income will go towards labor costs. For an employee, that's wages (30 percent of increased sales) and benefits (10 percent of increased sales). Keep in mind that to increase sales you will have to reduce your billable time, thus reducing your business's income. I'll cover finding and hiring good employees in Chapters 5 and 8.

Let's take a closer look at overhead expenses. For a typical consulting service business you should expect to spend about

40 percent of your income the first year and 25 percent in years after that. Where does it go? Rent will be about 10 percent of sales, office equipment and supplies will require another 5 percent, and your telephone about 5 percent. The remaining 20 percent the first year and 5 percent in subsequent years will go for advertising and promotion. The first year's advertising will cost more because you want to get your name out widely and because your advertising won't be as efficient. After the first year of advertising you'll know which media and messages work best for your market.

These estimates are guidelines to help you in calculating income, expenses, and profitability. As your business develops you may decide to make your salary a higher percentage of sales and reduce the profit or earnings you retain in the business. Or you may find that you can reduce expenses without reducing income by working from your home. Or you may decide to hire a spouse or friend even though it will increase your labor expense. There are many ways you can fine tune your budget. But, to start, stay as close to these percentages as possible. If you spend too little on rent, for example, your sales may be dramatically reduced because clients will judge you somewhat by the office you keep.

Minimizing Risks

Mark Twain noted, "There are two times in a man's life when he should not speculate: when he can't afford it, and when he can."

Certainly, there are many risks involved in starting and running your own business, no matter what type of business it is. But you can minimize these risks by understanding what you're getting into—the purpose of this book—and knowing how to get out of it if you must. Never enter a room without an exit. Chapter 8 will help you to discover those exits as well as help you to keep from using them.

A major risk to starting your consulting service is that you will lose your investment of time and money. How can you minimize these risks? Some consultants start their service at home in their spare time while working another job. This structure presents a number of challenges, but they can be overcome. The business can depend on an answering service or a relative to handle phone inquiries. In fact, depending on the needs of clients, a consulting service can turn this limitation to an advantage, by offering evening and weekend appointments that competitors do not.

The most successful consulting services are those which operate from a professional office shop near their clients. This can also be the most expensive operation as rent in a business district can be high. As a new consultant, you may be tempted to locate in a lower-rent area to reduce financial risks. Don't! You'll actually be increasing your financial risks because a poor location will yield a higher percentage of income going to rent. For example, a high-rent office may cost $1,200 a month but bring you $12,000 a month in business, costing 10 percent of income, whereas a $600-a-month office may only bring you $3,000 in business each month, costing 20 percent of income. The cheaper route can actually increase your risk.

An alternative to high rent is shared rent. That is, you may be able to sublease a desk or office from another business. This can be especially effective if the landlord offers a related but noncompeting service with which you can share clients. You'll be increasing income while you reduce risk. (I'll cover offices in greater detail in the next chapter.)

The best way to minimize risks is to understand what they are and prepare for those from which you cannot recover. You'll want fire insurance. You'll want sufficient operating capital to get you through the first 6 to 12 months of your business. You'll want only minimal office supplies. You'll want to come up with alternative services to ensure that you have income. You'll want to make sure that any leases you sign can be renegotiated if your business doesn't work out. As suggested earlier, make sure you have sufficient exits before you enter.

Action Guidelines

This introduction to starting your own consulting service has given you an overview of the business to help you determine if it is right for you. To help you make that decision, here are some actions you can take today:

✔ Start your consulting business notebook, writing down ideas and the answers to Action Guideline questions.

✔ List at least five potential consulting services you could furnish and indicate who might hire you to provide them.

✔ Check your local phone book's Yellow Pages under "Business Consultants," "Communication Consultants," "Insurance Consultants," "Real Estate Consultants," or other specific headings to see who your competition might be. Visit them.

✔ Read the business or appropriate classified section of newspapers in your area to determine who is offering consulting services and how they advertise.

✔ If possible, select one or two leading consulting services in your area and become a client.

✔ Do some rough calculations of your potential income and expenses based on guidelines in this chapter.

✔ Make a list of the risks you would face by starting your own consulting service.

✔ Talk to others about your ideas to get fresh prospectives on them.

REQUIREMENTS FOR CONSULTING SERVICES

C harles Schwab once said, "A man to carry on a successful business must have imagination. He must see things as in a vision, a dream of the whole thing." His words are true for both men and women who want to start a consulting service. Imagination is a major requirement.

What will you need to start and operate a successful consulting service? Certainly you will need your own special knowledge, skills, talent, some money, and some clients. But just as necessary is a personal desire to help others. This is important if you are an employee; it is vital if you are the owner. As a consumer, you can easily read the attitude of people who serve you. You know when someone is helping you because it's their job or because they enjoy doing their job. And clients usually respond by supporting and recommending those who help us solve our problems and make us feel important. They appreciate our business—and they get it.

Before you decide whether operating a consulting service is for you, you must know who *you* are. What do you feel most comfortable doing? Under what conditions do you enjoy working with people? Under what conditions do you prefer to avoid people? What are your personal goals? What are your financial goals? How much risk do you feel comfortable taking? Most important, is a consulting service a good fit in your life or will it cause more problems than it cures? Self-analysis can be difficult, but it is the only way of ensuring that this or any other goal will bring you the results you want in your life.

Your Personal Goals

Maybe by this stage in your life you've developed a list of personal goals for the next year, five years, and beyond. Most people have not. It isn't manditory that you develop a long list of your life's goals before you start a consulting service or other business, but it will increase your chances of personal and financial success.

These are questions to help you determine what you enjoy doing.

- What is it you want from your life?
- Do you have specific goals?
- What plans do you have for the next year of your life?
- Is there anything that people often compliment you about? A talent, hobby, or skill?
- Is there some work or task you would do even if you weren't paid?
- Is there some cause or mission that drives you?
- Is there some opportunity that strikes you as worthwhile?

A *goal* is an objective. It is somewhere you want to be or something you want to have. It can be the goal of owning your own consulting service. Or it may be the option of working at home. Or it can be amassing $1 million in assets within 20 years to fund your retirement. Whatever they are, they are your personal goals and they reflect who you are and what you want from your life.

Your Personal Values

Values are tools that will take you toward your personal goals. Values are standards or qualities that you've established to help you make daily decisions. Those people who succeed in any business have some common personal values. Let's look at those values together to determine your strengths and opportunities.

Self-awareness. The process of starting and operating any business is difficult. It will require that you constantly test yourself, maintaining what works and changing what doesn't. But that's what many people love about being a business owner: the endless challenges. It makes them aware of their characteristics and requires that they continue to grow.

Hard work. The great thing about being an independent businessperson is that you get to select which *12 hours* of the day you're going to work! It's true. As you start and grow your consulting business, you'll spend at least six hours a day producing your service and another two to eight hours marketing and administrating it. Don't expect to work just a 40-hour week— at least at first—and you won't be disappointed.

Discipline. Discipline is the power behind hard work. You can know exactly what needs to be done and still not do it. Self-discipline forces you to act. Having goals that are meaningful to you will increase your self-discipline.

Independence. Great business owners often make poor employees. They're too independent. That's all right. They cannot, however, be stubborn. Business owners must maintain a balance between independence and openmindedness to succeed.

Self-confidence. It takes a lot of nerve to start a business. It takes a lot more to make it successful. But nerve or self-confidence isn't ego. It's a belief in your unique skills founded on past success. You know you can successfully operate a consulting service because you have the skills to do so, not just the desire.

Adaptability. Life is chaos. No matter how much we plan, people and events change. Products change. Markets change. We change. A successful business owner must adapt to these changes. Without change, life becomes very dull.

Judgment. To succeed in business, you must make good decisions every day. Wisdom requires knowledge. You must be able to gather complete and accurate facts and make the best decision you can from those facts. You will not be right every time, but you will be right most of the time. This is good judgment.

Stress tolerance. Stress has been defined as "the confusion created when one's mind overrides the body's basic desire to clobber some yo-yo who desperately deserves it." Humor can help reduce stress. Stress is a part of everyday life, especially in business. Learning to live with stress without taking it personally can help you succeed in business.

Need to achieve. Success is the achievement of something you go after. It may be the completion of a project, or the start of a business, or the learning of a new skill. This need is a driving force within successful business owners that helps give them the energy to reach their goal.

In assessing your personal values, read Geoffrey Bellman's excellent book, *The Consultant's Calling: Bringing Who You Are to What You Do* (Jossey-Bass, 1990). It offers thought-provoking ideas on making consulting a way of life, balancing your work in your life, developing honest relationships with clients, and feeling good about making money.

Your Financial Goals

As much as you may love helping people, you must also have financial goals. Without a fair salary and profit, you won't be able to help people for very long.

What is an appropriate financial goal for your consulting service? One that funds your other goals. If your business goal is to open a new consulting service office each year for three years, your financial goal must be one that will fund such an ambitious goal. If your business goal is to build a successful consulting service then sell it in ten years and retire, your financial goal must match the expected selling price of your business. If your business goal is to make a good salary as well as a fair return on your investment, you must first determine what a good salary and a fair return mean to you.

One successful tax consulting service owner established a financial goal of developing annual sales of $200,000 within three years in order to take on a partner who could offer other financial services. He then wanted to spend two more years developing the single location—working the bugs out—before selling the business to the partner for enough to pay off his home's mortgage and do some traveling. His goals were specific and attainable.

Your Risk Tolerance

Business is legalized gambling. When you start a business you're gambling that you will succeed. You're also facing the risk that you will fail and face personal and financial loss. How much does this risk bother you? How much risk can you tolerate?

Everyone's risk tolerance level is different. Some people cannot afford to lose a dime. Of course, as they say in Las Vegas: "One who can't afford to lose, can't afford to gamble." Others say: "I started with nothing. Anything I get is a gain." Still others determine potential losses and say: "It's worth the gamble, but I'm going to do whatever I can to improve the odds."

You must determine your own risk tolerance and that of those with whom you share your life. If you're ready to take the plunge, but your spouse would rather not, find a mutually acceptable level of risk before starting your business. Otherwise, you may find, as too many people have, that you've traded an invaluable relationship for a replaceable business.

Tools and Equipment You Will Need

There are a variety of tools available that can make your consulting service more efficient and more profitable. They include computers, software, printers, copiers, reference books, answering machines, fax machines, desks, chairs, and stationery. Here's how successful consulting services select these vital tools.

Computer Hardware

A computer is one of the most valuable tools a consulting service can own. A computer can help you efficiently track information, manage prospects and clients, develop sales letters and marketing brochures, and manage your income and expenses. In most cases, you simply cannot operate a competitive consulting service without a computer anymore.

People are often apprehensive about computers because of all the new terminology that they must decipher: CPUs, bits, bytes, bauds, networks, boards, hard disks, RAM, monitor interlacing, and on and on. Don't worry about it. You'll quickly pick up what the terms mean. Here's a simplified introduction to computers—or it may be a review. Because most business computers are IBM-compatible, that's the type I'll discuss. Apple's Macintosh computers use a different operating system, but the basics are the same.

CPUs. A CPU is a central processing unit. It is an electronic machine built around a microprocessor called a *chip,* which processes information for you.

The CPU is typically called by the same name as the microprocessor chip that is its brain. For example, early PCs (personal computers) used a microprocessor chip called the 8088 (eighty eighty-eight). So they are known as 88s or by the IBM brand name for the model, the XT. The next generation microprocessor and CPU was the 80286, referred to as the 286 (two eighty-six) or by the IBM brand model, the AT. Then came the 386, the 486, and the 586 or Intel Pentium microprocessor and CPU.

The next number to remember in looking at CPUs is the *clock speed.* XT chips had a clock speed of about 5 MHz (mega or million hertz). By comparison, today's 486 and newer microprocessors have clock speeds of 50 MHz and more!

You'll also hear the terms SX and DX. Simplified, a 486DX has more processing power than a 486SX. A DX2 is faster than a DX, and a DX4 is even faster.

So all you really need to know about buying a PC is that a 486 is faster than a 286 or 386, a DX2 is faster than an SX or DX, and a clock speed of 66 MHz is faster than one that's 33 MHz. Fortunately, there's not more than a few hundred dollars difference between fast and super-fast.

Hard Disks. The hard disk drives in your PC can hold thousands of pages of information on its stacked disks (that look like miniature LP records stacked on a record player—if you remember what record players look like). The hard disk controller knows where to look for any information you've put into it, and it can give you the information in a fraction of a second.

The storage capacity of a hard disk is measured by the number of bytes or computer (not English) words that it can store. Actually, capacity is normally measured in millions of bytes, or megabytes (Mb). Older PCs were equipped with hard disks of 10Mb, 20Mb, or 40Mb. Newer PCs can store 120Mb, 240Mb, 500Mb or even one billion bytes, a gigabyte (Gb), or more. That's *one billion bytes.* To put that in terms that are more understandable, a 1Gb hard disk can theoretically store about a half-million typed pages.

RAM. A hard disk is a storage area, much like a library where millions of pieces of information can be kept. But a computer also needs a work area where information can be open and used. This place is called the *random access memory* or RAM.

Depending on the size of the programs you will be using, your PC's RAM should be at least 4Mb. Older PCs offered between $\frac{1}{2}$ and 1Mb of RAM, but today's PCs typically come with 4 to 32Mb. The larger this work area is, the more work that can be done simultaneously. Some software like Microsoft Windows and Novell NetWare require at least 4Mb and really work better if you have 8Mb of RAM or more.

Diskette Drives. Data can be moved from one PC to another using small, portable diskettes. These diskettes, sometimes called *floppies,* can store from a third of a megabyte to up to nearly three megabytes of information. Once you've developed a file on your hard disk, you can transport the data by instructing the PC to copy it to a diskette.

In the past ten years since PCs have become popular, a number of diskette formats of higher density have evolved. A higher density of magnetic particles allows storage of more information, once the computer's operating system has formatted the diskette. Earlier diskettes were 5¼ inches square, and were made of a thin, round plastic disk placed in a bendable (hence the name floppy) envelope and sealed. As technology has developed, a greater amount of information can now fit on one diskette. Early *single-density* diskettes held 360K (kilo or one thousand bytes), then *double-density* disks stored 720K. *High-density* quickly multiplied storage to 1,200K or 1.2Mb. Many PCs still use the 5¼-inch format.

Another format soon emerged, the 3½-inch diskette with a thin, round plastic diskette housed in a hard plastic case. Double-density 3½-inch diskettes hold 720K, and high-density diskettes store 1.44Mb. The newest format can store up to 2.88Mb of info on a diskette that will fit into a shirt pocket!

The storage capacity of a diskette is a function of the computer as well as the diskette. If you buy a used or older computer, make sure it can read high-density diskettes.

Another option is the removable hard drive. A couple of choices in this area are SyQuest or Bernoulli. They attach to your computer and allow you to store up to 44 or 88Mb of information onto a disk. The disk may be used to back up your data files. This is also an excellent method of storing older files that may be used again, rather than keeping them on your hard drive.

Monitor. You will also require a monitor, similar to a TV screen where the information you're working on is displayed. A monochrome (black and white) monitor is least expensive. Color monitors are easier to read—and more attractive—but also more expensive. SVGA (super video gate array) monitors are today's cost-effective standard. Rather than get into a boring description of interlacing and pixels, look for a quality monitor that's easy to read. If you can't see the difference between a $300 monitor and one that costs $1,000, don't buy the expensive one. Most monitors require that you buy a separate video card to be installed in the computer. Video cards also have random access memory, called VRAM, to help them display screens quickly.

Computer Software

Now that you understand the basics of computers, you can better see how computer programs work for you. And even though computer hardware is discussed here first, you will probably select the computer programs or software before you choose the computer or hardware to run it on.

A computer program is a set of instructions written in a language that your computer understands. The program can be as simple as a word processor or as complex as a database. Let's look at the function of each category of computer software.

Operating systems. DOS stands for disk operating system, which comes with your computer and translates commands like "copy" into a language that your PC understands. The most widely used DOS is MS-DOS developed by Microsoft Corp. Novell DOS was developed by Digital Research, now owned by Novell. IBM OS/2 is another popular operating system.

Shell programs make your PC easier to use and perform a number of important maintenance functions. It's called a shell because it wraps around the less friendly DOS program to make it easier to copy, delete, and manage files. Some shell programs also include *utilities* or special programs that help you keep your data organized and safe.

Windows is a program developed by Microsoft that lets you open a number of overlapping boxes or windows on your computer screen, each with different programs in them. You can be writing a letter when a client calls and you quickly switch to a window with information about the client and your current project.

Word Processors. Word processors simply process words. That is, they let you type words into the computer, move them around, insert words, take some out, and make any changes you want before you print them on paper. You can use word processors to write letters to clients and prospects. I've used computer word processors for more than ten years and would never go back to typewriters. Word processors let you change your mind.

Common word processing programs include WordPerfect, Microsoft Word, Ami Pro, WordStar, and XyWrite. Each has its own unique features and following. Some are more user-friendly than others. WordPerfect is one of the most widely used word processors. Ami Pro is probably the friendliest. Microsoft Word is popular for users of Microsoft Windows.

Spreadsheets. A spreadsheet arranges numbers into useable form. It's named after the wide multicolumnar sheets that accountants use to make journal entries. There are many ways you will soon find yourself using a spreadsheet software program.

As an example, you can purchase a basic spreadsheet program for about $100 that will let you enter horizontal rows or lines of job expense categories and vertical columns of numbers. Most important, you can then tell the program to make calculations on any or all of the columns or rows and it will do so in less than a second. If you update a number, it automatically recalculates the total for you.

Fancier and more costly spreadsheets can follow instructions you write, called *macros*, to do special calculations automatically. You may want to write a macro that will select all of the invoices over 60 days due and total them up. Better spreadsheets will also produce fancy graphs and pie charts that impress lenders and other financial types.

Popular spreadsheet programs include Lotus 1-2-3, Borland Quattro Pro, and Microsoft Excel.

Databases. A database software program is much like an index card file box. You can write thousands or even millions of pieces of information and store them. But a database program is even better than a file box because it finds information in the files in a fraction of a second.

The most common application of a database program for consulting services is a client file. If you only have a few clients, this may not be necessary. But as you add clients, prospects, and other business contacts, you may soon need at least a simple database program to keep track of them. You can also develop a database of resources, by category, and sell this information to your clients.

Your prospect/client database will keep information about their name, street address, city, state, zip code, phone and fax numbers, contact names, annual budget information, list of projects you've completed for them, information about their business, and even their hobbies. Then, if you want to find out how many of your clients are located in a specific city and haven't purchased any services from you in the last year, you simply tell your database program to search its files for you. It's that easy.

Popular database programs include Borland Paradox, Microsoft Access, Lotus Approach, and Microsoft FoxPro. Depending on which word processor and spreadsheet you select, you may want to purchase a database program by the same company. For example, if you use Lotus's Ami Pro and 1-2-3, consider their database program, Approach. The operating logic of each software developer is slightly different from that of other developers, but you'll usually see continuity within product lines.

Integrated Programs. You can also find integrated software programs that combine the three primary programs: word processor, spreadsheet, and database. Ask your local computer store to recommend a good integrated program. Some include other related programs, such as communications software that lets your PC talk to other PCs over the phone using modems. The cost of a good-quality integrated system is usually much less than the total price for the individual components.

Here's another plus to integrated programs: They talk to each other. That is, your word processor can include financial figures from your spreadsheet in your correspondence, and send it by modem to someone listed in your database. Just as important, an integrated group of programs developed by a single software firm will have similar commands in each program. You won't have to learn three separate programs, you'll learn one larger program.

Integrated programs are especially recommended for those who don't want to spend a lot of time selecting and learning numerous software programs. Popular integrated programs include Microsoft Works, ClarisWorks, Lotus SmartSuite, Borland Office, and Microsoft Office.

Vertical Software. In addition to general word processors, there are software programs developed to help specific businesses and industries. They include job estimating software for contractors, traffic systems for radio and television stations, design programs for illustrators, desktop publishing systems for publishers and printers, scheduling programs for project managers, and many others.

Printers

Letters and other business documents must be sent from your computer to a printer to be printed on paper. There are many types of printers to select from. But we only need to cover the basics of them here so you'll know which ones to look for as you go shopping.

Dot Matrix. The dot matrix printer forms letters from a bunch of dots. A 9-pin printer uses nine tiny pins—three rows of three—to form each letter. The 24-pin printer does the same job but uses 24 pins—four rows of six. So the letters formed by a 24-pin printer are easier to read than that of a 9-pin printer. Today, most dot matrix printers use 24 pins.

Laser. A laser is simply a beam of light that's focused by a mirror. A small laser in your printer actually writes the characters by magnetizing a piece of paper, black dust called toner is passed over it and sticks to the places the laser light touched, then the sheet travels through a heater that fuses the black toner to the paper. An LED or light-emitting-diode printer works in virtually the same way with less wear on the system.

Bubble Jet. Similar to the laser, the bubble jet printer sprays special ink onto the page in patterns cut by heat. Bubble jet printers are typically less expensive than laser printers.

Which type of printer should you buy? If you are only printing standard correspondence, a simple bubble jet printer will probably serve your needs. If you require large engineering drawings, you will shop for a special printer called a plotter. If you are doing some publishing or want your reports to look as good as they can, shop for a medium-resolution (600 dpi) laser printer.

Copiers

Copy machines can be very useful to your consulting business, especially if you don't have a PC and a printer. You will want to conveniently copy correspondence, plans, proposals, contracts, agreements, procedures, and other business documents. A good copier can be purchased for under $800. If you're producing a client newsletter, your own brochures, direct mail pieces, or other marketing documents, your copy machine can be more cost-effective than running down to the copy shop or printer for a few copies every day.

Features you will want to look for in a copier may include enlargement and reduction, paper trays, collating of multiple copies, and reproduction of photos. Depending on what consulting services and related products you sell, you may want a copier that can produce duplex or two-sided copies. Or you may want a copier that prints on 11 x 17-inch sheets for professional four-page consulting services. Determine your copying needs before you buy.

Fax Machines

There are more than 25 million fax machines in the world, with most of them installed in businesses. The concept of the fax machine is simple: it reads a sheet of paper for dark spots much like a copy machine does. It then converts these spots into a code that's sent across a telephone line at a speed of nearly 10,000 bits of information per second. Based on international standards, the fax machine on the other end knows how to read these signals and convert them into light and dark spots that conform to the image that was sent. This image is printed on a piece of paper, and you have a facsimile or fax.

The consultant can now send letters, proposals, sales letters, literature, copies of invoices, and other printed material to prospects, clients, and others in just seconds. A typical one-page fax takes less than a minute to transmit on a Group 3 fax machine. Group 3 is the current standard for facsimile machines established by an international committee for data communication, the CCITT. The fax machine, like the computer, is dramatically changing the way that businesses conduct business.

Facsimile machines look like small printers with a tray to hold outgoing paper and a telephone set either attached or nearby. You call a fax number, and your fax machine sends out a tone that tells the other fax machine it would like to transmit a facsimile. The receiving machine sends your machine a high-pitched tone, you manually press your machine's start button and hang up the phone. The fax is being transmitted. Some machines automate the process; you simply put the copy into the machine, press a button that calls a specific telephone in memory, and the fax is sent without any outside help.

There are dozens of features to consider when buying a fax machine for your business. However, many are frills. Most important is that your fax machine is Group-3 compatible. Beyond that, explain to the salesperson what you need your fax machine for and let him or her show you the newest features and whistles. You can get a basic fax machine for $300 to $400, a better one for $400 to $800, and your heart's desire for a thousand dollars or more. Or you can rent or lease a fax machine. This is an especially good idea with products like faxes that quickly become obsolete.

The more expensive fax machines will print on plain paper rather than slick thermal paper that has a tendency to curl and fade. Depending on how you use documents faxed to you and how long you keep them, a plain paper fax may or may not be most economical.

Some fax machines you look at will combine other functions. It may have a standard telephone handset that you can use for your primary or secondary business line. Some also include a tape or digital answering machine. This setup is practical because you have the business phone line feeding into one machine that can serve three purposes: lets you answer, takes messages, and takes and sends faxes. But, like any machine that combines functions, if one goes out or becomes obsolete, they may all go. Compare the cost of a combined unit against the cost of individual units. If there is little difference in total cost, go for the separate components.

If you decide to purchase a computer for your consulting business, consider PC fax boards. They are printed circuit boards that are installed inside your computer and allow you to plug in a phone and use it as a fax. There are even models that will serve as your answering machine as well. Fax boards are typically purchased through computer stores. Computer software can let you fax letters, proposals and other documents directly from your computer without printing them first to paper.

Telephone Service

Businesses have a number of telephone service options available to them. The most popular is the 800 number, available through most long-distance telephone companies. Having an 800 number allows your prospects and clients to call you toll-free. You pay for the call. The advantage is that more people will be inclined to call you. That's also the disadvantage as salespeople will use it to pitch you—on your dime! Toll-free 800 service is available through most long-distance carriers for a small monthly charge plus a per-minute charge that is slightly higher than standard long-distance rates. Call your carrier for more information and fees on 800 service.

Two new telephone services include 700 service and 500 service. Marketed under various trade names, the 700 service lets calls follow subscribers anywhere within 127 countries and areas. If you work from a variety of offices, a 700-prefix telephone number can be useful as the people who need to reach you will be able to. There is typically an enrollment fee and a monthly fee for the service. For more information on 700 service, call AT&T EasyReach at 800-982-8480, or your preferred long-distance carrier.

A 500-prefix telephone number, a new service, automatically routes incoming calls to various locations you select: office, cellular, home, etc. If not picked up at any of the locations, a voice mailbox takes a message from the caller. For more information on 500 service, call AT&T True Connections at 800-870-9222, or your preferred long-distance carrier.

Reference Books

There are many valuable reference books to help you manage your consulting business. They include titles on your specialty (advertising, pensions, records management, beauty and fashion, retirement planning, writing, etc.) as well as general books on business and resources:

- *Accounting* by Peter Eisen (Barron's Business Review Series, 1990)
- *Dictionary of Business Terms* by Jack P. Friedman (Barron's Business Guides, 1987)
- *How to Make a 1,000 Mistakes in Business and Still Succeed* by Harold L. Wright (The Wright Track, 1990)
- *Lesko's Info-Power II,* by Matthew Lesko (Information USA, 1994)
- *Management* by Patrick J. Montana and Bruce H. Charnov (Barron's Business Review Series, 1993)
- *Marketing* by Richard L. Sandhusen (Barron's Business Review Series, 1993)
- *The Vest-Pocket Guide to Business Ratios* by Michael R. Tyran (Prentice-Hall, 1992)
- *The Vest-Pocket Marketer* by Alexander Hiam (Prentice-Hall, 1991)
- *The Business Planning Guide, Sixth Edition* by David H. Bangs, Jr. (Upstart Publishing, 1992)
- *The Information Please Business Almanac and Desk Reference* edited by Seth Godin (Houghton-Mifflin, 1994)

Office Supplies

Depending on the type of consulting services you offer, office supplies will vary. At a minimum you will want notepads, pens, pencils, a calculator, paper clips, and related items. If you have a computer and printer you will also want copy paper for drafts and quality paper for correspondence and proposals.

A computer will also require preformatted diskettes, tapes (if your PC has a tape drive for backing up data files), cleaners, and other supplies.

Your office will need furniture, storage cabinets, chairs, and related equipment, especially if you will be bringing clients into your office.

Primary Information Resources

You will be selling qualified advice to those who can profit from it. To develop good advice, you will need to keep up on the latest information within your chosen fields. This means buying books, subscribing to magazines, and interviewing experts.

Of course, this book can't advise you on all of the primary information resources for your specialty. However, you are probably aware of most of them already. If not, reading books and subscribing to primary trade journals in the specific field will give you most of them. Membership in related trade associations will bring you the rest of them.

Depending on your specialty, you can take advantage of the 8,000 free experts on almost any topic available through the federal government. Refer to Chapter 38 of *Lesko's Info-Power II* by Matthew Lesko (Information USA, 1994) for a listing, by subject, of these experts on everything from ABS resins to zoris. Listed are the location and telephone numbers for experts on hospital care statistics, county business patterns, facilities management, gem stones, aging population, computer networks, knitting machines, pulp mills, runaway youth, and literally thousands of other topics. Lesko's book has more than 1,500 pages of such resources.

Calculating Financial Requirements

How much money will you need to build a profitable consulting service? Figure 2.1, on page 41, will help you make a preliminary estimate of your business's financial requirements. These estimates will be revised and expanded in future chapters.

To estimate start-up costs you will need to make your best guess of how much it will cost to set up your office for the day you open the front door to your first client. This includes the cost of preparing and equipping your office, getting required licenses and professional memberships, getting the phone hooked up, and funding your initial advertising.

Estimating operating costs can be more difficult because it requires that you estimate your living expenses. Most people who have been employees spend as much as they make; they're not sure exactly what they *need* to live on. However, by starting with your current net (after taxes) salary, you can roughly calculate whether you require more or less to live on. If you operate your business as a sole proprietor (discussed further in Chapter 4), your income taxes and self-employment (social security) tax will be paid by the business.

Other operating costs are those expenses that you will pay each month to keep the doors open (fixed or overhead expenses) as well as those that increase as sales increase (variable expenses).

Consultant and author Alan Weiss suggests that a new consultant should calculate start-up requirements as:

- one year of living expense,
- plus 10 percent contingency,
- plus six months of office expenses,
- plus any special equipment expenses.

From this, the new consultant can deduct:

- cash and securities on hand,
- plus Accounts Receivable,

Financial Worksheet

Estimated Start-Up Costs:

Office preparation	$_____
Office equipment	$_____
Initial office supplies	$_____
Telephone, answering machine	$_____
Utility deposits	$_____
Licenses & permits	$_____
Insurance	$_____
Professionals	$_____
Signs	$_____
Initial advertising	$_____
Miscellaneous expenses	$_____
Total Estimated Start-Up Costs	$_____

Estimated Operating Costs:

Living expenses	$_____
Employee salaries	$_____
Rent	$_____
Utilities	$_____
Advertising	$_____
Insurance	$_____
Office supplies	$_____
Taxes	$_____
Equipment maintenance	$_____
Total Estimated Operating Costs	$_____

Estimated Financial Resources:

Assets

Checking and savings	$_____
CDs and securities	$_____
Owed to you	$_____
Real estate	$_____
Autos and vehicles	$_____
Insurance cash value	$_____
Other assets	$_____
Total assets	$_____

Liabilities

Credit cards	$_____
Household credit	$_____
Auto loans	$_____
Taxes	$_____
Education loans	$_____
Mortgages	$_____
Other liabilities	$_____
Total liabilities	$_____
Total net worth	$_____

Figure 2.1: Financial worksheet for calculating your businesses start-up, operating costs, and financial resources.

- plus contracted but unbilled business,
- plus credit line access.

For example, if you need $40,000 to live on for the next year, add $4,000 as contingency. If office expenses are estimated at $2,000 a month, add in $12,000 to cover the first six months, and, if $4,000 is needed for a computer and office furniture, the initial capital requirements are $60,000. If you have $15,000 in cash, $5,000 in money owed to you, and another $25,000 in work contracted but not completed yet, you still need $15,000. A credit line of at least $15,000 or a loan for the same amount will theoretically give you sufficient funds to start and operate your consulting business through the first year.

Where can you get the money you need to start your business? A survey of small businesses conducted by Coopers & Lybrand found that 73 percent were funded by the owners and their families, 13 percent by outside investors, 8 percent by banks, and 6 percent by alliances with other businesses. However, the survey reported that the businesses that were owner-financed had the highest failure rate. You'll learn how to use your financial resources—and develop new ones—in Chapter 7.

Skills You Will Need

Do you have what it takes to own and manage a professional consulting service? Besides the personal goals and values discussed earlier in this chapter, there are specific skills that are necessary to make your business profitable.

First, you must be a people person. That is, you must enjoy working with and for people. You don't have to like each one, but you do have to find common ground on which you can have a professional relationship of service. You must remember that the client may not always be right, but he or she is always the client. And the client pays your bills.

You will need specific knowledge of your field, expertise within one or more disciplines, special skills required for your trade, and contacts that can furnish you with information and with clients.

As there are hundreds of specializations within the consulting trade, the specific skills you will need within your specialty must be listed and developed by you. As a starter, look at your potential competitors. What skills do they have? Which skills do they promote? What skills do you have that they may not?

Time Management Tips

How can the consulting service business owner ensure that his or her time is well managed? First, by organizing work space so that important papers don't get lost and unimportant papers do. You can also make a rule that you will avoid handling papers more than once. If you pick up a piece of paper, make a decision regarding it right then if possible.

Set up a regular work schedule. It may be from 7 A.M. to 6 P.M. or 8 P.M. to 5 P.M., or 6 A.M. to 6 P.M. Whatever it is, try to stick to it. If you manage your time well, you will be able to. If you have one time of the day that seems more productive for you than others, plan your most important functions around it.

What about travel and waiting time? Take work with you in a briefcase or purchase a laptop computer that you can use to keep productive every minute. As your time management skills improve you'll learn how to do more than one thing at a time. You could be making job notes or talking with a key employee or gathering information on an upcoming project while you're waiting to talk with a client.

Meetings seem to be one of the biggest time-wasters there are. But you can change this by thoroughly preparing for all of your meetings. Meetings, to be productive, must have a purpose or an agenda and a time limit. Even if you didn't call the meeting, if you see that it has no focus or structure you can step in and say, "I have another appointment in an hour. What topics do we have to cover in that hour?" then list those topics as the agenda.

One more time management tip: Use one of the popular time management planning systems to help you get the most out of your day. They include Day Timer (Day Timers, Inc.; 800-225-5005), Day Runner (Harper House, Inc.; available in stationary stores) and Planner Pad (Planner Pads, Inc.; 402-592-0666). These and other systems give you a place to record appointments, daily to-do lists, special projects and their steps, as well as a contact book for names and addresses. If you spend most of your time in the office at a computer, there are numerous contact management and scheduling programs that will help you manage your time. If you use a portable computer, you can install these programs and carry this information wherever you go.

A simple daily planner is illustrated in Figure 2.2, on page 46. Figure 2.3, on page 47, is a useful form for recording daily things to do. Figure 2.4, on page 48, illustrates a handy monthly planner.

Time and stress are closely related. The lack of time to do what you need to do often increases personal stress. How do you manage both? Following are ideas from a successful consultant.

- Plan your time and establish priorities on a daily "to do" list.

- Decide what your prime time is and do your most important or difficult tasks then.

- Set business hours, specific times when you're at work and times when you turn on the answering machine because you're on duty but off call. You, your clients, and your family will appreciate knowing your set routine, even though you know that for special events or emergencies you can break that schedule.

- Confirm your appointments one-half day before the appointment—in the afternoon for next morning or morning for that afternoon. It will save you time, and your clients will appreciate the consideration.

- If you're working from your home, give your business as much of a separate and distinct identity as possible. Although you might save a few dollars by using the dining room table as a desk and a cardboard box as a file cabinet, the stress and strain of operating without proper space and supplies will take its toll.

- Have a separate room or area for your business, with a separate entrance if clients visit. Consider sound-proofing so your family won't be bothered by your noise and vice versa. In addition to the psychological and physical comfort of having a separate room for your home office, the IRS requires it in order for you to make a legitimate claim for tax deductions.

		DAILY PLANNER

AAA Consulting

DAY OF THE WEEK:

MONTH AND YEAR: Dec 1994

TIME	TO DO	NOTES
8:00 - 9:00	Meet with Henderson Building Materials staff	
9:00 - 10:00		
10:00 - 11:00	Call Jeff Upstart on Borland project	
11:00 - 12:00	Prepare for Jefferson meeting	
12:00 - 1:00	Lunch with Rotary	Ask Frank about Nelson Tires
1:00 - 2:00	Stop by Miller Paints to pick up contract	
2:00 - 3:00	Jones -555-8765	
3:00 - 4:00	Everett Hardware - 555-2345	
4:00 - 5:00	Thornton Travel - 555-5432	
5:00 - 6:00	Review day and plan tomorrow	
6:00 - 7:00		
7:00 - 8:00	Dinner party at Jason Thompson's	
8:00 - 9:00		
9:00 - 10:00		
10:00 - 11:00		
11:00 - 12:00		

Figure 2.2: Daily planner is useful for organizing your work day.

AAA Consulting

Things To Do

Date: June 5, 1995

1 Meet with Jim Johnson about Carter Real Estate account

2 4:00 p.m. conference call with Bill Stephens

3 Lunch meeting with Jane Miller

4 Design new advertising campaign

5 Review May financial statements

6

7

8

9

10

11

12

Figure 2.3: By prioritzing your daily tasks, you can ensure that the most important ones are tackled first.

AAA Consulting

Monthly Activity Planner

PERSON: Bill Smith
FROM: July 1, 1995
TO: July 31, 1995

PRIORITIES	Monday	Tuesday	Wednesday	Thursday	Friday	Saturday	Sunday
1 Orient new employee	Introduce Bob Review job	Staff mtg @	Review	Call accounts	Meet with Bob	Golf with Frank	
2 Purchase new computer	Demonstrations		Jake's PCs @ 3pm	CompWorld @ 11am			
3 Train employees on new computer		Windows class 9-10am	WordPerfect 1-2pm	Accounting 3-4pm		Theirtown	Theirtown
4 Market new services	Theirtown		Shopper ad mgr @ 10am	Newspaper ad mgr @ 11am		Golf	Golf
5							

Figure 2.4: Use your monthly planner to plan important projects and events.

Action Guidelines

You've learned the requirements of starting and operating a successful consulting service. They include evaluating your personal and financial goals as well as your tolerance for risk; reviewing the tools you need; calculating financial requirement; assessing the skills you will need to be successful; and learning how to efficiently manage your time. Here's how to implement what you've learned in this chapter.

✔ Using your consulting business notebook, make notes regarding your personal goals and values, your financial goals, and your tolerance for risk. Be as honest as possible.

✔ Plan your purchase of a computer, printer, and software for your consulting service. Don't buy it yet; just start learning what you can about them.

✔ Start gathering your reference library. Look at your current bookshelf for primary reference books you have as well as those you know you will need.

✔ Complete the financial worksheet in this chapter to determine how much you'll need and where you can get it.

✔ List the skills you'll need to enhance or add to make your consulting service successful. How can you develop or improve on these skills?

✔ Select and use a time-management system if you don't already.

✔ Review your consulting service requirements and start thinking about resources, the topic of the next chapter.

RESOURCES FOR CONSULTANTS

A resource is a person, product, or service that can help you reach your objectives. Resources for your consulting service include your own experiences, your prospective clients, trade associations, conventions, seminars, training courses, books, magazines, and governmental offices. Together they can increase your working knowledge of consulting services and business as well as help you understand how to work efficiently and profitably.

This chapter offers information on these and other resources. Included are addresses and telephone numbers when appropriate to help you get your consulting service off the ground.

Your Own Experiences with Consulting Services

The first and most important resource for your consulting service is you. Your experiences with consulting services may be limited to working within a specific trade or purchasing a consumer product or service in the past. Or maybe you don't have extensive experience with consulting services, but you do have skills that would be valuable to businesses or consumers.

The point is that to serve your clients well you must understand their needs. You must know how they feel, what they need, how they buy, and how they use the advice you sell them. The best experience you can have is as someone who previously hired or used the services of consultants.

Take time to review your own experiences with con-sulting services. Consider what advice you have received as well as what advice you would have like to receive.

- Which of your own decisions have been successful and which have not?

- Was there any specific advice or resources that seemed to work best?

- If you have hired consultants in the past, what did you look for in them?

- Did you have a problem for which you would have paid well for a solution?

- Is there some advice you have received from others that you feel has been invaluable to you?

- List five or six elements that, in your experience, must be included in an effective consulting service.

In any business, success requires empathy and empathy requires experience. The more you understand about your client, the better you will be able to serve him or her.

What Do Your Clients Need?

The best way to understand your clients is to interview them. Find out what they are thinking. Understand what they want from a consulting service and from you. Ask them what is most important to them. Learn what makes them select one consulting service over another.

How can you interview clients before you start your consulting service? By interviewing prospective clients or prospects. Talk with friends or business contacts who have recently solicited advice on specific topics. Set up a part-time consulting service, such as on weekends, and interview people who respond to your ad.

In general, you'll learn that your clients want an effective consulting service that offers advice of greater value than the cost. Depending on your chosen clientele, the next most important requirement may be price, speed, or quality. They may need to have a solution that costs less than $500 or within 24 hours or one that will multiply their investment by at least 20. You may learn that two of these three elements—price, speed, quality—are already served in your area and that there is a sufficiently large market for consulting services that are developed for the third element.

Chapter 6 will cover marketing in greater detail. For now, work toward an understanding of your potential clients' needs.

Trade Associations for Consultants

A trade association is a group of businesses that agree to share information among themselves regarding their trade. Plumbers have them, car makers have them; so do consultants.

There are dozens of trade associations for consultants listed in the *Encyclopedia of Associations* (Gale, 1994). There are associations for bridal consultants, acoustical consultants, merger and acquisition consultants, professional writing consultants, computer consultants, airport consultants, insurance management consultants, and many others. Check your local library for a recent edition of *Encyclopedia of Associations*.

A few of the trade associations for consultants include:

- American Association of Professional Consultants (3577 Fourth Ave., San Diego, CA 92103)
- American Consultants League (1290 Palm Ave., Sarasota, FL 34236; 813-952-9290)
- Association of Management Consulting Firms (521 5th Ave., New York, NY 10175; 212-697-9693)
- Institute of Management Consultants (19 W. 44th St., New York, NY 10036; 212-697-8262)

In addition, membership in the American Management Association (135 W. 50th St., New York, NY 10020; 212-586-8100) may be useful.

Conventions and Seminars for Consultants

Many professional associations and marketing groups sponsor annual conventions of members and professionals. Workshops, guest speakers, and roundtables are organized to encourage consultants from across the country to share information, techniques, and ideas. Associations (addresses above) that sponsor conventions include Association of Management Consulting Firms, American Association of Professional Consultants, and American Consultants League.

Books for Consultants

There is a wide shelf of books written to help consultants ply their trade. Besides the one you're reading, they include:

- *How to Make It Big As a Consultant, Second Edition* by William A. Cohen (AMACOM, 1991)
- *Million Dollar Consulting: The Professional's Guide to Growing a Practice* by Alan Weiss (McGraw-Hill, 1992).

- *Start and Run a Profitable Consulting Business, Third Edition* by Douglas A. Gray (Self-Counsel Press, 1990)
- *The Consultant's Calling: Bringing Who You Are to What You Do* by Geoffrey M. Bellman (Jossey-Bass Inc., 1990)
- *The Independent Consultant's Q & A Book* by Lawrence Tuller (Bob Adams Inc., 1992)

Magazines and Trade Journals for Consultants

It pays to stay up-to-date with the latest in trends and news. Below are a few of the best magazines and journals for consultants.

- *ACME Newsletter* (Association of Management Consulting Firms (521 5th Ave., New York, NY 10175; 212-697-9693)
- *Consultants News* (Kennedy & Kennedy Inc., Templeton Rd., Fitzwilliam, NH 03447; 603-585-2200)
- *Consulting Intelligence* (American Consultants League, 1290 Palm Ave., Sarasota, FL 34236; 813-952-9290)
- *Independent Consultant's Briefing* (313-449-0310).
- *The Consultant's Voice* (American Association of Professional Consultants, 3577 Fourth Ave., San Diego, CA 92103)

Consulting Service Opportunities

A *business opportunity* is an arrangement by which someone who has found success in a specific business teaches you how to do the same. A business opportunity is different from a franchise in that requirements for offering a franchise, and the related fees, are much higher than for an opportunity. Depending on the opportunity, you may be licensed to use their name in your advertisement. A supplier will furnish you with a product that you can then resell to your clients.

There are a number of consultants who specialize in helping other consultants. One is Hal Wright of The Wright Track (P.O. Box 3416, Oak Park, IL 60303; 800-779-6093). Mr. Wright specializes in assisting consultants who help small businesses grow.

Franchising is a form of licensing by which the owner (the franchisor) of a product or service distributes through affiliated dealers (the franchisees). The franchise license is typically for a specific geographical area. The product or service is marketed by a brand name (McDonalds, Chevrolet), and the franchisor controls the way that it is marketed. The franchisor requires consistency among the franchisees: standardized products or services, trademarks, uniform symbols, equipment, and storefronts. The franchisor typically offers assistance in organizing, training, merchandising, and management. In exchange, the franchisor receives initial franchise fees and an ongoing fee based on sales levels.

There is a wide variety of franchises available for those who want to sell advice to others. They include wedding consulting, financial and investment planning, shipping consultants, stock sales, building inspection, small business consulting, accounting services, and many more franchise opportunities.

One useful source of information on available franchises is the *Franchise Opportunities Handbook* produced and published by the United States Department of Commerce and available through the Superintendent of Documents (U.S. Government Printing Office, Washington, DC 20402) or your regional federal bookstore. This handbook lists basic information on franchises available in 44 categories including the name and address of the franchisor, a description of the operation, number of franchises, how long the franchise has been in business, how much equity capital is needed, how much financial assistance is available, what training is provided, and what managerial assistance is available.

Another source of information on franchises is the International Franchise Association (1350 New York Avenue N.W., Suite 900, Washington, DC 20005). The IFA's *Franchise Opportunities Guide* is a comprehensive listing of franchisors by industry and business category. *Franchising Opportunities* is their bimonthly magazine. Their newsletter, *Franchising World*, includes information on developing trends in franchising.

Other sources include *Entrepreneur*, *Income Opportunities*, and other magazines available on most newsstands.

Small Business Administration Resources

Founded more than 40 years ago, the U.S. Small Business Administration or SBA (1441 L Street N.W., Washington, DC 20416) has offices in 100 cities across the U.S. and a charter to help small businesses start and grow. The SBA offers counseling, booklets on business topics, and administers a small business loan guarantee program. To find your area's SBA office, check the White Pages of metropolitan telephone books in your region under "United States Government, Small Business Administration."

The SBA also operates the Small Business Answer Desk, a toll-free response line (800-827-5722) that answers questions about SBA services. In addition, it sponsors the 13,000 Service Corps of Retired Executives (SCORE) volunteers, Active Corps of Executives (ACE) volunteers, Business Development Centers, and Technology Access Centers.

The SBA offers numerous publications, services, and videos for starting and managing small businesses. Publications are available on products/ideas/inventions, financial management, management and planning, marketing, crime prevention, personnel management, and other topics. The booklets can be purchased for one or two dollars each at SBA offices or from SBA Publications, P.O. Box 30, Denver, CO 80201. Ask first for SBA Form 115A, The Small Business Directory, that lists available publications and includes an order form.

Another popular service is SBA On-Line, a computer bulletin board operated by the Small Business Administration. It receives more than 1,000 calls a day and has handled one million calls since it opened in 1992. Once you're familiar with computers and modems, you can access this resource by having your system call 900-463-4636. There is a small fee for its use, currently about $6 an hour. The bulletin board includes extensive resources for small businesses and access to other government agencies. If you want to access a limited version of this popular bulletin board, dial 800-697-4636. It doesn't have as many resources, but it is free.

The Service Corps of Retired Executives (SCORE; 1441 L Street N.W./Room 100, Washington, DC 20416) is a national nonprofit association with a goal of helping small businesses. SCORE is sponsored by the SBA and the local office is usually in or near that of the local SBA office. SCORE members, retired men and women, and ACE members, still active in their own business, donate their time and experience to counseling individuals regarding small business.

The 700 Business Development Centers (BDCs) are regional centers funded by the SBA and managed in conjunction with regional colleges. A BDC offers free and confidential counseling for small business owners and managers, new businesses, home-based businesses, and people with ideas concerning retail, service, wholesale, manufacturing, and farm businesses. BDCs sponsor seminars on various business topics, assist in developing business and marketing plans, inform entrepreneurs of employer requirements, and teach cash flow budgeting and management. BDCs also gather information sources, assist in locating business resources, and make referrals.

Small Business Institutes are partnerships between the SBA and nearly 500 colleges offering counseling services to area businesses. SBIs conduct market research, develop business and marketing plans, and help small businesses work out manufacturing problems. Contact your regional SBA office to find out if a local college has such a program. You could get free or low-cost assistance from the college's business faculty and students.

Tax Information Resources

The U.S. Treasury Department's Internal Revenue Service offers numerous Small Business Tax Education Program videos through their regional offices. Topics include depreciation, business use of your home, employment taxes, excise taxes, starting a business, sole proprietorships, partnerships, self-employed retirement plans, Sub-Chapter S corporations, and federal tax deposits.

If you're considering using a portion of your home as a business office, request *Business Use of Your Home* (Publication 587) from the Internal Revenue Service (Washington, DC 20224). It's free and will help you determine if your business qualifies for this option as well as how to take advantage of it to lower your taxes.

Depending on how much you use your business vehicle for personal use, you can either list all costs of operating the vehicle as an expense or you can deduct a standard mileage rate as an expense when you file income taxes. For more information, request *Business Use of a Car* (Publication 917) from the Internal Revenue Service. There's no charge for this publication. Figure 3.1, on page 60, is a worksheet for calculating your business mileage deduction.

What business expenses are deductible? There's a long list. The best answer is found in a free publication offered by the Internal Revenue Service, *Business Expenses* (Publication 535).

AAA Consulting	AUTOMOBILE TRAVEL LOG
	Monthly Summary Sheet
	Date:

AUTOMOBILE INFORMATION

Make of Auto: Lexus

Year & Model: 1993

Vehicle I.D. Number: 1234567890

Driver of Vehicle: Bob Simmons

Odometer   End of month: 12,345.00

                            Beginning of month: 11,111.00

Total Miles Driven: 1,234.00

Qualified Business Miles Driven: 1,234.00

Allowable Reimbursement Rate: 1,234.00   x $ 0.28 /mi

                          Total Expense $ $345.52

YEAR TO DATE - INFORMATION

	BUSINESS MILES	TOTAL MILES
Prior YTD	5,678	5,678
Current Month	1,234	1,234
New YTD	6,912	6,912

DATE: _____   SIGNATURE : _____

                                     APPROVAL : _____

Figure 3.1: Automotive mileage driven for business purposes is a legitimate expense. Keep track of mileage with a a travel log such as this one.

You can choose to deduct in one tax year a limited amount of what you spend to acquire certain tangible property for use in your business instead of treating the amount as a capital expense. The maximum amount you can deduct is currently $17,500. Called a Section 179 deduction after the IRS ruling, it allows you to treat a purchase as an expense rather than as a capital expenditure subject to depreciation. For example, a $10,000 computer system can be written off as an expense in a single year rather than depreciated at $2,000 a year for five years.

Action Guidelines

There is a wide variety of resources available to professional consultants including your experiences, prospective clients, trade associations, conventions, seminars, training courses, books, magazines, suppliers, and governmental offices. Here's how to put them to work for you.

✔ Review your own experiences with consulting services as well as the experiences of friends, family and business associates.

✔ Make notes in your consulting business notebook on what you feel your prospective clients need and want from a consulting service.

✔ Start calling and writing for catalogs and information from resources.

✔ Begin purchasing reference books and subscribing to trade journals that you will use in your consulting service.

✔ Review your list of skills and needs then find training resources to enhance them.

✔ Contact franchisors to determine costs and benefits of buying a franchise or opportunity.

✔ Contact your regional SBA and BDC offices to learn how they can help you start and build your business.

✔ Contact the IRS for booklets, forms, and other resources.

STARTING UP YOUR CONSULTING SERVICE

B y now, you've learned what a successful consulting service does, studied the resources available to you, and decided that you want to start your own consulting business. You're ready to put your sign out and find your first client.

Not yet. Before you start your consulting service you must first plan to make it a success. You don't want to close up shop in six months because you misjudged the local market or overspent your income. Instead, you want to celebrate your first anniversary looking back on a successful year and looking forward to many more.

This chapter will help you plan for your success, then execute that plan to ensure that your consulting business will be profitable.

Will Your Consulting Service Succeed?

The adage that businesses don't plan to fail, they just fail to plan is accurate. Without a plan for your business, you may soon find yourself in a venture that neither satisfies your needs nor pays your bills.

A business plan is a document that can be used both by people contemplating going into business and those already in business. A business plan helps you focus your thoughts and ideas, summarizing your product, your process, your market, and your expectations into a single document that can guide you in your daily decisions as well as help you develop financing for start-up and expansion.

An excellent guide for creating a successful business plan is David H. Bangs Jr.'s best-seller *The Business Planning Guide, Sixth Edition* (Upstart Publishing). It offers clear, step-by-step procedures for pulling a business plan together for a consulting service or any other business venture. It includes worksheets, resources, and a sample business plan.

Your business plan will answer these five questions:

1. How much money do I need?
2. On what will the money be spent?
3. Who will own and who will operate the business?
4. What are the projected financial results of the business?
5. Do I really know enough about this business?

If your business plan is intended to develop financing through a bank or a backer, it must also answer the question: How will the funds be repaid?

Your business plan will include a statement of purpose, an outline of your product or service, a discussion of your clients and how you will reach them, as well as current and projected financial information.

A typical consulting service may develop a statement of purpose that reads:

> AAA Bridal Consulting Service will offer cost-effective wedding consulting. Start-up requires $10,000 in cash from savings for equipment, rent, supplies, and a salary for the first two months of operation until the business is expected to be profitable.

If you're using the business plan to develop financing, it will be more developed and specific than the plan you would write to guide you through the first year of operation. In addition, a business plan for a $10,000 start-up is typically shorter than one for a $100,000 expansion project.

Selecting Your Business Name

Naming a business is much like naming a baby. In some ways, it will give direction to its growth. A well-named business will seem more successful to prospects and will then become so.

Consultant Hal Wright suggests that the word "Consulting" should not be in the business name as it is frequently overused. In any case, a business name should make it clear to prospects what the firm does, or at least the industry the firm is in. Here are some examples:

- Midtown Investment Services (describes the location and the product)
- Sandra's Wedding Planning Service (identifies the product, but is personalized at the expense of sounding like a small business)

- Henderson Financial Strategies, Inc. (sounds bigger; surnames are better than first names and Inc. implies that it is a larger firm—but can be used only if your business is incorporated.)
- AAA Shopping Services (specifically identifies the service and assures first-listing in alphabetical directories such as the Yellow Pages)
- Smithtown Services (unclear what service is involved)
- Quality Pension Service (clearly identifies the product and the owner's attitude)

In selecting a business name, many firms write a defining motto or slogan (Figure 4.1, on page 67) that's used in all stationery and advertisements to further clarify what the firm does:

- Specializing in helping you plan your successful retirement.
- We can help you find your dream home.
- Low-cost investment opportunies.
- Helping your business grow.
- Let's look into the future together.
- Helping you plan your health care.
- Specializing in business acquisitions.

An assumed business name is a name other than the real and true name of each person operating a business. A real and true name becomes an assumed business name with the addition of any words that imply the existence of additional owners. For example, Bob Smith is a real and true name, while Bob Smith Company is an assumed business name.

In most states and counties, you must register an assumed business name (d.b.a. or "doing business as") to let the public know who is transacting business under that name. Without the registration you may be fined or, worse, not be able to defend a legal action because your assumed business name

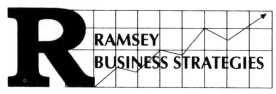

Helping your business grow

Figure 4.1: A definitive business name and slogan can effectively communicate your image to prospects and customers.

wasn't properly registered. Most assumed business name registrations also require a fee, which is usually small.

In many states, an assumed business name is registered with the state's corporate division. Some states will also register your assumed business name with counties in which you do business. Other states require that you do so. In some locations, you must publish a public notice in an area newspaper telling all that you (and any other business principals) are operating under a specific business name.

The typical assumed business name registration requires the following information: the business name you wish to assume, the principal place of business, the name of an authorized representative, your SIC code (standard industrial classification; for a consulting service, it is 8742-11), a list of all owners with their signatures, and a list of all counties in which your firm will transact business (sell, lease, or purchase goods or services; receive funding or credit). Specialized consultants, such as consulting engineers or career planners, have their own SIC numbers, available from American Business Lists (402-331-7169).

Locating Your Business

Where will you locate your consulting service? The answer depends on how much business you expect to initially earn, what your space requirements are, your budget, and whether you plan to have clients visit your place of business.

Here are some points to consider as you decide where to locate your business:

- Proximity to your primary clients
- Opportunities for signage
- Availability of transportation
- Requirements and availability of parking facilities
- Cost of operation
- Tax burden
- Quality of police and fire services
- Environmental factors
- Physical suitability of building
- Opportunities for future expansion
- Personal convenience

The first and most important consideration is making sure that you are located conveniently for your clients. The best locations for consulting services are near colleges, universities, trade schools, business schools, employment offices, or in major business districts, depending on your primary clientele. Considering these factors, let's look at your options.

Home Office

Approximately 30 percent of all consulting services operate exclusively from home offices. Many others start at home and move to business offices as they grow. The entrepreneur sets up a small office at the dining table, in a walk-in closet, an extra bedroom, or a shop. This is an ideal situation for a part-time consulting service for many reasons. First, there will be little or no additional rent expense. It is also more convenient for you to have all your records at home, where you can review them at any time. In addition, you could ask a family member or someone living with you to answer the telephone while you're away. Finally, you can legally deduct some of your household costs as legitimate expenses and reduce your tax obligation.

But the best reason is that it saves you time. A client can call you in the evening to ask about a specific job and you can quickly check your records or make notes in the job file without leaving your home. The most popular initial location for a home-based consulting service is a desk in a spare room.

Of course, with a home office you will want to discourage walk-in clients. Don't include your address in your ads. Rather, have prospects call you to set up an appointment. Make sure that the path from your front door to your office is short and looks as professional as possible. Clients are hiring you for your professionalism as well as your consulting services skills.

Remember, though, operating a consulting service from your home is typically only temporary and only for part-time businesses. Once you've developed a clientele and are ready to make your business full-time, seriously consider a commercial location.

Professional Office

As your consulting services business grows, you will want to move to your own office. The biggest disadvantage of such a move is the cost. But there are many advantages. First, your own office will give you an image of being a large, successful, and permanent firm. Second, your business requires that prospects, clients, or others come to your office. An office of your own will give them a better first impression. Third, it will give you control over your business that you cannot have if you're working out of a spare bedroom.

Many business consulting services prefer to locate in professional office centers with other services that serve the business community: attorneys, employment agencies, copy shops, desktop publishing services. Especially consider professional office centers that have well-known clients and will encourage foot traffic.

Shopping Mall

Consumer consulting services typically don't locate in a shopping mall because of the high costs. However, many take advantage of the mall's traffic by renting a professional office on a mall's second floor or in a satellite office complex next to a popular mall. There are many types of shopping malls: neighborhood, community, regional, and super-regional.

A neighborhood shopping center is built around a supermarket or drugstore with a trade population of 2,500 to 40,000 and offers 30,000 to 100,000 square feet of leasable space.

A community shopping center (100,000 to 300,000 square feet) often has a variety or discount department store as its leading tenant and serves a trade population of 40,000 to 150,000.

A regional shopping center (300,000 to 1,000,000 square feet) builds around one or more full-line department stores with a trade population of 150,000 or more.

A super-regional shopping center includes three or more department stores with more than 750,000 square feet of leasable space.

Selecting a Location

As mentioned, the most important factor in selecting a retail location is retail compatibility. For your small business in its early years of operation, with limited funds for advertising and promotion, locating your business near a traffic-generator can help you survive. You'll often find restaurants grouped together. Competing antique stores may take over a city block.

The old business adage says that the three most important factors in selecting a retail site are location, location, and location.

The next most important factor in selecting your retail site is the availability of a local merchants association. A strong merchants association can accomplish through group strength what an individual store owner couldn't even dream of. A merchants association cannot only speak as a booming voice to city planners, buy also bulk-buy advertising at lower rates and promote its own events. But make sure that you understand your responsibilities to the association before you sign up. If the site you select doesn't have a merchants association, consider starting one.

Other factors include the responsiveness of the landlord, and the opportunities for negotiating a favorable lease. Make sure your new landlord is continuing to invest in the property including regular maintenance and quick repairs. And talk with other commercial landlords in your area to ensure that your lease is the best you can negotiate.

You can often get assistance on selecting a retail site by talking with local and regional chambers of commerce about your needs. They may be able to give you an educated guess on what you will probably have to pay for a property that will help your business become successful.

Zoning Laws

Your consulting business location may be limited by local zoning laws. Before deciding where you will set up your business, talk to the local zoning office about restrictions. You may find that so-called cottage or home businesses are allowed in your neighborhood as long as clients don't park on the street.

The Americans with Disabilities Act (ADA) requires that business owners offer access to their location that does not restrict employees or clients with disabilities. This act applies to all businesses with 15 or more employees.

Employment Laws You Must Know About

As you consider adding employees to your business, there are certain laws, federal and state, that come into play. Your local state employment office can assist you in learning the current requirements of these laws.

- The Social Security Act of 1935, as amended, is concerned with employment insurance laws as well as retirement insurance.

- The Fair Labor Standards Act of 1938, as amended, establishes minimum wages, overtime pay, record keeping, and child labor standards for most businesses.

- The Occupational Safety and Health Act (OSHA) of 1970 is concerned with safety and health in the workplace and covers almost all employers. There are specific standards, regulations, and reporting requirements that must be met.

There are other laws that may concern your business. Contact your local state employment office to determine the requirements for hiring disadvantaged workers, federal service contracts for work on public buildings or other public projects, employee pension and welfare benefit plans, and the garnishment of an employee's wages.

In addition, the Immigration Reform and Control Act of 1986 prohibits employing illegal aliens. Employers must require every employee to fill out the Employment Eligibility Verification Form (Form 19) within three days of the date of hire (if hired after November 7, 1987). Fines are levied for noncompliance. For more information, contact the nearest office of the Immigration and Naturalization Service.

The Civil Rights Act of 1964 prohibits discrimination in employment practices because of race, religion, sex, or national origin. Public Law 90-202 prohibits discrimination on the basis of age with respect to individuals who are between 40 and 70 years of age. Federal laws also prohibit discrimination against the physically handicapped. Again, your state employment office can help you in understanding the laws regarding applicants and employment. In addition, firms like G. Neil (720 International Parkway, Sunrise, FL 33345) offer catalogs of human relations supplies: job applications, personnel folders, labor law posters, attendance controllers, employee awards, and related materials.

Forms of Business

One of the most important decisions you will make as you start your consulting services business is what legal form it will take. Why so important? Because how you record expenses, how you build your business, how you pay taxes, how you treat profits, and how you manage liability all depend on the structure you give your business.

Of course, as your business grows, you'll be able to move from one type of structure to another, but sometimes there will be a cost. The cost will be paid to the tax man as he decides whether you changed structure to avoid paying your fair share of taxes. One of the reasons you may later change structure is because you want to legally reduce tax liability— and that's okay. It's the abuse of tax laws that brings the wrath of the IRS.

There are four common types of business structures: proprietorship, partnership, corporation and, a relatively new structure, the limited liability company. Each has specific advantages and disadvantages, but they must all be considered against your individual circumstances, goals, and needs.

Proprietorship

A sole proprietorship is a business that is owned and operated by one person. However, in many states a business owned jointly by a husband and wife is considered a proprietorship rather than a partnership. This is the easiest form of business to establish. You only need to obtain required licenses and begin operation. For its simplicity, the proprietorship is the most widespread form of small business organization and is especially popular with the new consultant.

The first and most obvious advantage of a proprietorship is ease of formation. There is less formality and fewer legal restrictions associated with establishing a sole proprietorship. It needs little or no governmental approval and is less expensive to start than a partnership or a corporation.

Another advantage of a proprietorship is that it doesn't require that you share profits with anyone. Whatever is left over after you pay the bills (including the tax man) is yours to keep. You will report income, expenses, and profit to the IRS using Schedule C and your standard 1040 form, and make quarterly estimated tax payments to the IRS so you don't get behind before your annual filing.

Control is important to the successful consulting business. A proprietorship gives that control and decision-making power to a single person, you. Proprietorships also give the owner flexibility that other forms of business do not. A partner must usually get agreement from other partners. In larger matters, a corporation must get agreement from other members of the board of directors or corporate officers. A proprietor simply makes up his or her mind and acts.

One more plus: the sole proprietor has relative freedom from government control and special taxation. Sure, the government has some say in how you operate and what taxes you will pay. But the government has less to say to the sole proprietor.

Yes, there's a downside to being the only boss. Most important is unlimited liability. That is, the individual proprietor is responsible for the full amount of business debts, which may exceed the proprietor's total investment. With some exceptions, this liability extends to all the proprietor's assets, such as house and car. One way around this is for the proprietor to obtain sufficient insurance coverage to reduce the risk from physical loss and personal injury. But if your suppliers aren't getting paid, they can come after your personal assets.

When the business is a single individual, the serious illness or death of that person can end the business.

Individuals typically cannot get the credit and capital that partnerships and corporations can. Fortunately, most consulting services don't require extensive capital. But when they do, they seriously consider the advantages of taking on a partner or becoming a corporation.

Finally, as a sole proprietor you have a relatively limited viewpoint and experience because you're only one person. You're more subject to tunnel vision or seeing things in a narrow way based on your experiences. You don't have someone with a commitment to your business who can give you a fresh viewpoint or new ideas.

Partnership

The Uniform Partnership Act (UPA), adopted by many states, defines a partnership as "an association of two or more persons to carry on as co-owners of a business for profit." How the partnership is structured, the powers and limitations of each partner, and their participation in the business are written into a document called the Articles of Partnership. The articles or descriptions can either be written by the partners, found in a legal form from a stationery store, or written by an attorney. Obviously, using an attorney is the best option because it will ensure that the document is binding and reduce disputes that typically come up once the business is growing.

Your firm's Articles of Partnership should include:

- the name, location, length, and purpose of the partnership,
- the type of partnership,
- a definition of the partners' individual contributions,
- an agreement on how business expenses will be handled,
- an outline of the authority of each partner,
- a summary of the accounting methods that will be used,
- a definition of how profits and losses will be distributed among the partners,
- the salaries and capital draws for each partner,
- an agreement of how the partnership will be modified or terminated, including dissolution of the partnership by death or disability of a member or by the decision of partners to disband, and
- a description of how the members will arbitrate and settle disputes as well as change terms of the partnership agreement.

Partnerships are easier and less costly to form than corporations. In most states, all that's really needed are the Articles of Partnership.

A partnership can typically raise capital more easily than a proprietorship. This is because there are more people whose assets can be combined as equity for the loan. Lenders will look at the credit ratings of each partner, so make sure that your business partners have good credit.

Partnerships are frequently more flexible in the decision-making process than a corporation, but less flexible than a proprietorship.

Like proprietorships, partnerships offer relative freedom from government control and special taxation. A partnership doesn't pay income tax. Rather, all profits and losses flow through the partnership to the individual partners who pay income and other taxes as if they were sole proprietors.

Of course, there are some minuses to partnerships. Like sole proprietorships, at least one partner will be a *general partner* and will assume unlimited liability for the business. A general partner should obtain sufficient insurance coverage to reduce the risk from physical loss or personal injury, but the general partner is still liable.

A partnership is as stable or as unstable as its members. Elimination of any partner often means automatic dissolution of the partnership. However, the business can continue to operate if the agreement includes provisions for the right of survivorship and possible creation of a new partnership. Partnership insurance can assist surviving partners in purchasing the equity of a deceased partner.

Though a partnership has less difficulty in getting financing than a sole proprietorship, the fragile nature of partnerships sometimes makes it difficult to get long-term financing. The best source, as discussed earlier, is using the combined equity of the partners from assets they own as individuals. In fact, many partnerships are started because an active partner needs equity or financing that he cannot get without a partner with more assets or better credit.

Depending upon how the partnership agreement is drawn up, any partner may be able to bind all of the partners to financial obligations. Make sure your Articles of Partnership accurately reflects your intent regarding how partners can or cannot obligate the partnership. Also consider the advantages and disadvantages of structuring your partnership as a limited liability company, discussed in this book right after corporations.

A major drawback to partnerships is the difficulty faced when arranging the leaving of a partner. Buying out the partner's interest may be difficult unless terms have been specifically worked out in the partnership agreement.

As you can see, there are numerous pluses and minuses to partnerships. Many of the disadvantages can be addressed in your Articles of Partnership. This is why it is recommended that you use an attorney experienced in such agreements as you construct your partnership. The cost is usually less than the value.

Corporation

Businesses, as they grow, often become corporations (technically called C corporations), identified by an extension to their name: Corp., Inc., or, in Canada, Ltd. A corporation is usually formed by the authority of a state government. The steps to forming a corporation begin with writing incorporation papers and issuing capital stock. Then, approval must be obtained from the secretary of state in the state in which the corporation is being formed. Only then can the corporation act as a legal entity separate from those who own its stock.

The primary advantage to incorporation is that it limits the stockholder's liability to their investment. If you buy $1,000 of stock in a corporation and it fails, you can only lose up to the $1,000 investment. The corporation's creditors cannot come back to you demanding more money. The exception is when you put up some of your own assets as collateral for the corporation.

Ownership of a corporation is a transferable asset. In fact, the New York Stock Exchange and other exchanges make a big business out of transferring stock, or partial ownership, in corporations from one investor to another. If your consulting services business is a corporation, you can sell partial ownership or stock in it within certain limits. In fact, this is how many corporations get money to grow. A corporation can also issue long-term bonds to gain cash required to purchase assets or build the business.

Your corporation has a separate and legal existence. Your corporation is not you or anybody else. It is itself. For example, in the case of illness, death, or other cause for loss of a corporate officer or owner, the corporation continues to exist and do business.

The corporation can also delegate authority to hired managers, although they are often one and the same. Thus you become an employee of the corporation.

Corporations have disadvantages, too. The corporation's state charter may limit the type of business it does to a specific industry or service. However, other states allow broad charters that permit corporations to operate in any legal enterprise.

Corporations face more governmental regulations on all levels—local, state, and federal. That means your business will spend more time and money fulfilling these requirements as a corporation than it would as a proprietorship or a partnership.

If your corporate manager is not also a stockholder, he will have less incentive to be efficient than he would if he had a share in your business.

As you can imagine, a corporation is more expensive to form than other types of businesses. Even if you don't use an attorney, there are forms and fees that will quickly add up. However, an attorney is a good investment when incorporating your consulting services business.

Finally, corporations allow the federal and some state governments to tax income twice: once as corporate net income and once as it's received by the individual stockholders in the form of salary or dividends. A Sub-Chapter S corporation allows small businesses to tax the business as if it were a sole proprietorship or partnership (no corporate income tax) and pass the tax liability on to the individual stockholders. There are about 1.6 million Sub-Chapter S corporations in the U.S. Recent changes in the law may make it easier to get financing for a Sub-S. Talk with an attorney or accountant about this option.

Limited Liability Company

Similar to a partnership, a limited liability company (LLC) is taxed only once on its profits. A C corporation, as mentioned, is taxed twice. Unlike a partnership, an LLC protects partners by limiting their personal liability for actions of the company. An LLC offers liability protections similar to a corporation. In addition, LLCs have fewer restrictions on shareholders and allow the transfer of shares more easily than a corporation. Finally, profits are reported on personal rather than corporate tax returns.

LLCs must be privately held companies. While restructuring a C corporation into an LLC can be difficult and costly, changing your business from an LLC to a C corporation is quite easy. One major drawback to LLCs is that their limitation of liability has not been extensively tested in the court system, as has that of corporations. If you decide to establish an LLC, make sure you have an attorney who has experience with this structure and who can advise you based on liability and tax issues in your state.

About 40 states recognize limited liability companies as a legal business structure. They have been popular in other countries for many years. In establishing an LLC you will need to file articles of organization and an operating agreement with state authorities. For more information on LLCs, contact the Association of Limited Liability Companies (202-965-6565).

A Guide to Limited Liability Companies is available from Commerce Clearing House (800-835-5224).

How to Hire an Attorney

To find an attorney who is familiar with business of your size and trade, ask for a referral from a business colleague, your banker, your accountant, your local chamber of commerce, or other business services in your area. Many local bar associations run an attorney referral and information service; check your local telephone book's Yellow Pages under "Attorneys' Referral & Information Services." Some referral services give you only names and phone numbers; other actually give information on experience and fees to help you match your needs to the attorney's background and charges.

An attorney can help you decide which is the most advantageous business structure for you. He or she can also help you with zoning, licensing problems, unpaid bills, contracts and agreements, employment laws, copyright questions, trademarks, and some tax problems.

Because there is always the possibility of a lawsuit, claim, or other legal action against your business, it is wise to have an attorney who is already familiar with your business lined up before a crisis arises. An attorney with experience serving employment service businesses can also advise you on federal, state, and local laws, programs, and agencies to help you prepare for or prevent potential problems.

Let your attorney know that you expect to be informed of all developments and consulted before any decisions are made on your behalf. You may also want to receive copies of all documents, letters, and memos written and received regarding your project. If this isn't practical, you should at least have the opportunity to read such correspondence at your attorney's office.

How to Hire an Accountant

Many new consulting services fail because of poor financial management. Sometimes the best decision a new business owner makes is to hire the services of a public accounting firm. An accountant can design record-keeping systems, set up ways for maintaining records, analyze financial information, and help you relate that information to profitability.

Daily bits of information will flow into your consulting services business. As you serve clients, you will generate information about sales, cash, supplies, purchase expenses, payroll, Accounts Payable, and, if credit is offered to clients, Accounts Receivable.

To capture these facts and figures, a system is necessary. If you don't feel comfortable with setting up and managing such a system, don't be shy about hiring an accounting service. An accountant can help design one for recording the information that you need to control finances and make profitable decisions.

Once a system of records has been set up, the question is: Who should keep the books? The accounting service who has set up the books may keep them. However, if you have a general understanding of record keeping you can do them yourself and save some money. Use your accountant for checking and analyzing your records. Once your business has grown, you may want to hire someone to keep your records and perform other office functions.

In addition to record keeping, an accountant can advise you on financial management, providing you with cash flow requirements, budget forecasts, borrowing, business organization, and tax information.

By analyzing cash flow requirements, an accountant can help you work out the amount of cash needed to operate your firm during a specific period—for example, three months, six months, the next year. He or she considers how much cash you will need to carry client Accounts Receivable, to buy equipment and supplies, to pay current bills, and to repay loans. In addition, an accountant can determine how much cash will come from collection of Accounts Receivable and how much will have to be borrowed or pulled from an existing line of credit. While working out the cash requirements, your accountant may notice and call your attention to danger spots, such as accounts that are past due.

If you're applying for a loan, your accountant can assemble financial information, for example, a profit-and-loss or income statement and a balance sheet. The purpose of such data is to show the lender the financial position of your business and its ability to repay the loan. Using this information, your accountant can advise you on whether you need a short-term or long-term loan. If you have never borrowed before, your accountant may help you by introducing you to a lender who knows and respects the accountant's reputation. This, alone, may be worth the cost of hiring an accountant.

Taxes are another area in which an accountant can contribute advice and assistance. Normally, a record-keeping system that provides the information you need for making profitable decisions will suffice for tax purposes. However, if you purchase equipment that requires special depreciation, have employees who handle cash or require payroll taxes, or have extensive bad debts, a good accountant can help you identify the problems, suggest a method of keeping good records, and help you minimize your tax obligation by writing off bad debts as a business expense. Accounting firms will also get your federal and state withholding numbers for you, instruct you on where and when to file tax returns, prepare tax returns, and do general tax planning for your small business.

In looking for an accountant, get referrals from trusted friends, business associations, professional associations, and other business services. Discuss fees in advance and draw up a written agreement about how you will work together. Your accountant is your key financial adviser. He or she should alert you to potential danger areas and advise you on how to handle growth spurts, how to best plan for slow business times, and how to financially mature and protect your business future from unnecessary risk.

How to Hire an Insurance Professional

A good insurance agent is as valuable to your success as any other professional consultant. An experienced and trustworthy insurance agent can both reduce your exposure to risk and keep your insurance costs to a minimum.

Ask around among other business services and professionals for recommendations of a good insurance agent. If possible, search for one who primarily serves the business community rather than the family or individuals. They will better know your problems and concerns.

Ask prospective agents for some advice on a specific problem. Don't tell them what you think the solution is. Their responses can help you determine who is better at cost-effective problem solving.

The agent is the insurance industry's primary client representative. Typically, the independent agent is a small business owner and manager. By using this distribution system, insurance companies are represented by agents who receive a commission for selling the companies' products and services. An independent agent may represent more than one insurance company.

Liability insurance coverages, particularly for property damage and bodily injury, usually include legal defense at no additional charge when the policyholder is named a party to the lawsuit that involves a claim covered by the policy. Litigation is costly, whether the claimant's suit is valid or frivolous. The legal defense provision greatly reduces these costs to you.

Action Guidelines

Starting up your florist service requires a number of important steps: testing your business idea, estimating start-up costs, selecting your business name, locating your business, choosing the form of your business, and selecting your professional advisors. Here's how to implement what you've learned in Chapter 4.

✔ Start writing your business plan. Refer to *The Business Planning Guide,* by David H. Bangs, Jr., and other resources for worksheets and examples.

✔ Write your business's statement of purpose.

✔ Select your business name and find out how to register and protect it.

✔ Develop a slogan or motto that best fits your business.

✔ Decide where to initially locate your business. Research and consider many locations, writing information in your floral business notebook.

✔ Start designing your florist service shop: storefront, salesroom, workroom, receiving-shipping.

✔ Contact your state employment office and other government offices regarding employment laws and requirements. Also let them know about your services.

✔ Decide which form of business you will initially use: proprietorship, partnership, corporation, or limited liability company.

✔ Find a good attorney.

✔ Find a good accountant.

✔ Find a good insurance agent.

OPERATING YOUR CONSULTING SERVICE

S tarting a consulting service is only part of your goal. To succeed you must manage its daily operation. You must control operating costs, keep and analyze records, price and produce effective consulting services, hire and manage employees, and pay taxes.

This chapter covers these and other responsibilities of your consulting service's daily operations as suggested by successful business men and women. It will help you understand and focus on the nuts and bolts of your business as you keep your eyes on the broader purpose of your venture: to help others as you help yourself.

Estimating Your Operating Costs

Managing your consulting services business requires that you manage your business budget so you can continue to provide service, support, and employment to others as well as a profit to yourself. When you first started your business, you established a preliminary budget. Now that your business is operating, you must establish an operating budget.

A budget is a forecast of all cash sources and cash expenditures. It is organized in the same format as a financial statement, and most commonly covers a 12-month period. At the end of the year, the projected income and expenses in the budget are compared to the actual performance as recorded in the financial statement.

A budget can greatly enhance your chances of success by helping you estimate future needs and plan profits, spending, and overall cash flow. A budget allows you to detect problems before they occur and to alter your plans to prevent those problems.

In business, budgets help you determine how much money you have and how you will use it, as well as help you decide whether you have enough money to achieve your financial goals. As part of your business plan, a budget can help convince a loan officer that you know your business and have anticipated its needs.

A budget will indicate the cash required for necessary labor and materials, the day-to-day operating costs, the revenue needed to support business operations, and expected profit. If your budget indicates that you need more revenue than you can earn, you can adjust your plans by

- reducing expenditures (hiring independent contractors or part-time, rather than full-time, employees, purchasing less expensive furniture, eliminating an extra telephone line),
- expanding sales (offering additional services, conducting an aggressive marketing campaign, hiring a salesperson), and/or
- lowering your salary or profit expectations.

There are three main elements to a budget: sales revenue, total costs, and profit.

Sales are the cornerstone of a budget. It is crucial to estimate anticipated sales as accurately as possible. Base estimates on actual past sales figures. Once you target sales, you can calculate the related expenses necessary to achieve your goals.

Total costs include fixed and variable costs. Estimating costs is complicated because you must identify which costs will change—and by how much—and which costs will remain unchanged as sales increase. You must also consider inflation and rising prices as appropriate.

Variable costs are those that vary directly with sales. Paper and printer toner expenses are examples of variable costs for your consulting services business. Fixed costs are those that don't change regardless of sales volume. Rent is considered a fixed cost, as are salaries. Semivariable costs, such as telephone expenses, have both variable and fixed components. Part of the expense is listed as fixed (telephone line charges), and part is variable (long-distance charges).

Profit should be large enough to make a return on cash investment and your labor. Your investment is the money you put into the firm at start-up and the profit that you have left in the firm (retained earnings) from prior years. If you can receive 10 percent interest on $10,000 by investing outside of your business, then you should expect a similar return when investing $10,000 in equipment and other assets within the business. In targeting profits, you also want to be sure you're receiving a fair return on your labor. Your weekly paycheck should reflect what you could be earning elsewhere as an employee.

Establishing an Operating Budget

As you develop your budget, you'll be working with the budget equation. The basic budget equation is:

$$\text{Sales} = \text{Total Costs} + \text{Profit}$$

This equation shows that every sales dollar you receive is made up partly of a recovery of your costs and partly of profit. Another way to express the basic budgeting equation is:

$$\text{Sales} - \text{Total Costs} = \text{Profit}$$

This equation shows that, after reimbursing yourself for the cost of producing your service, the remaining part of the sales dollar is profit. For example, if you expect $1,000 for a specific job and you know that it will cost $900 to market and perform this service, your profit will be $100.

In calculating an operating budget, you will often make estimates based on past sales and cost figures. You will need to adjust these figures to reflect price increases, inflation, and other factors. For example, during the past three years, a consultant spent an average of $1,500 on advertising costs per year. For the coming year, the owner expects an advertising cost increase of 5 percent (0.05). To calculate next year's advertising costs, the owner multiplies the average annual advertising costs by the percentage price increase ($1,500 X 0.05 = $75) and adds that amount to the original annual cost ($1,500 + $75 = $1,575). A shortcut method is to multiply the original advertising cost by one plus the rate of increase ($1,500 X 1.05 = $1,575).

If your consulting services business is a new venture and has no past financial records, rely on your own experience and knowledge of the industry to estimate demand for and costs of your service. Your accountant or trade association may also be able to help you develop realistic estimates.

Before you create an operating budget, you must answer three questions:

1. How much net profit do you realistically want your business to generate during the calendar year?

2. How much will it cost to produce that profit?

3. How much sales revenue is necessary to support both profit and cost requirements?

To answer these questions, consider expected sales and all costs, either direct or indirect, associated with your consulting services. To make the safest estimates when budgeting, many companies overestimate expenses and underestimate sales revenue.

Start constructing your budget with either a forecast of sales or a forecast of profits. For practical purposes, most small businesses start with a forecast of profits. In other words, decide what profit you realistically want to make and then list the expenses you will incur to make that profit.

How to Keep Good Records

Why keep records? There are many reasons. For the individual just starting a consulting services business, an adequate record-keeping system increases the chances of survival. Established consulting services also can enhance their chances of staying in business and earning increasing profits with a good record-keeping system.

Keeping accurate and up-to-date business records is, for some people, the most difficult and uninteresting aspect of operating a business. If this area of business management is one that you believe will be hard for you, plan now how you will handle this task. Don't wait until tax time or until you're totally confused. Take a course at a local community college, ask a volunteer SCORE representative, or hire an accountant

Here are some of the questions that good business records can answer:

- How much business am I doing?
- How much credit am I extending?
- How are my collections?
- What are my losses from credit sales?
- Who owes me money? Who is delinquent?
- Should I continue extending credit to delinquent accounts?
- How much cash do I have on hand?
- How much cash do I have in the bank?
- Does this amount agree with what records tell me I should have, or is there a shortage?
- How much have I invested in supplies?
- How often do I turn over my supplies inventory?
- How much do I owe my suppliers and other creditors?
- How much gross profit or margin did I earn?
- What were my expenses? What's my weekly payroll?
- Do I have adequate payroll records to meet the requirements of workers' compensation insurance, wage-and-hour laws, social security insurance, unemployment compensation insurance, and withholding taxes?
- How much net profit did I earn?
- How much income tax will I owe?
- Are my sales, expenses, profits, and capital showing improvements or did I do better last year than this?
- How do I stand as compared with two periods ago?
- Is my business's position about the same, improving, or deteriorating?
- On what services am I making a profit, breaking even, or losing money?
- Am I taking full advantage of cash discounts for prompt payments?
- Are the discounts I get from suppliers as great as those I give to my customers?
- How do the financial facts of my florist service business compare with those of similar businesses?

to advise you on setting up and maintaining your record-keeping system. Another option is to trade your specialized consulting services with a professional accountant client.

Your records will be used to prepare tax returns, make business decisions, and apply for loans. Set aside a special time each day to update your records. It will pay off in the long run with more deductions and fewer headaches. A good record-keeping system should be:

- simple to use,
- easy to understand,
- reliable,
- accurate,
- consistent, and
- timely.

Several published systems and software systems provide simplified records, usually in a single record book. These systems cover the primary records required for all businesses; some are modified specifically for the consulting services business. Check your local office supply store, your trade association, or trade journals for more information on specialized record books.

Simply, your records should tell you these three facts:

1. How much cash you owe
2. How much cash is owed to you
3. How much cash you have on hand

To keep track of everything, you should have these basic journals:

- A sales journal shows the business transaction, date, for whom it was performed, and the amount of the invoice
- A cash receipts register (Figure 5.1, on page 94) shows the amount of money received, from whom, and for what.

AAA Consulting			**Cash Receipts Register**		
				PERIOD ENDING: May 30 1995	

Date	Check Number	Account Number	Amount	Name	
May 2 1995	4321	9876	$2,500.00	Jefferson Tool and Die - Retainer for May	
May 7 1995	6543	8765	$1,100.00	Smith Motors - On account	
May 11 1995	2109	6565	$3,200.00	Billings & Billings - Hillary project	

Figure 5.1: Typical cash receipts journal.

- A cash disbursements register (Figure 5.2, on page 96) or check register shows each check disbursed, the date of the disbursement, number of the check, to whom it was made out (payee), the amount of money disbursed, and for what purpose.

- A general journal for noncash transactions and those involving the owner's equity in the business.

In addition, here are other records you will need in your business:

- Accounts Receivable is the record of accounts on which you are due money from a sale for which you haven't been fully paid.

- Accounts Payable is the record of accounts for which you will have to pay money because you have purchased a product or service but haven't paid for it all.

- Inventory record is a record of your firm's investment in paper, envelopes, books, videos, and other items you intend to resell.

- Equipment is a record of your firm's investment in equipment that you will use in providing your service and will not normally resell.

- Payroll is a record of the wages of employees and their deductions for income, FICA, and other taxes as well as other payroll deductions.

Some businesses combine all of these journals into a single journal. In fact, there are many good one-write systems available that allow you to make a single entry for each transaction. You can also use computer software such as Quicken, Quick-Books, Microsoft Money, or Manage Your Money to track income and expenses in a checkbook format. More extensive accounting software programs include Peachtree Accounting and M.Y.O.B. (Mind Your Own Business).

AAA Consulting			Cash Disbursements Register		
			PERIOD ENDING: May 30 1995		
Date	Check Number	Account Number	Amount		Name
May 1 1995	1234	5678	$850.00	Johnson Realty - Lease payment	
May 3 1995	1235	9876	$243.00	AT&T - Telephone bill	
May 5 1995	1236	3210	$790.00	Bradford Secretarial Services - Temporary help	
May 8 1995	1237	7654	$3,000.00	Bob Simmons - Capital draw	

Figure 5.2: Typical cash disbursements journal.

Single Entry or Double Entry?

There are two ways to record transactions in your business: with a single entry or with a double entry. The primary advantage to single-entry record keeping is that it is easy. As the name implies, you make a single entry that records the source of each income or destination of each expense. Each entry is either a plus or a minus to the amount of cash that you have. Receipt of a check on an outstanding account is a plus. Payment of a supplies order is a minus. As long as you have a limited number of transactions, single-entry accounting is adequate.

But as your consulting service grows in complexity, you will want a check-and-balance system that ensures that records are accurate. Double-entry accounting requires that you make two offsetting entries that balance each other. A check received on an outstanding account is a debit to Cash and a credit to Accounts Receivable. Payment for a supplies order is a debit to Supplies and a credit to Cash.

Every account has two sides: a left or debit side and a right or credit side. The posted debits must always equal the posted credits. Some types of accounts are called debit accounts because their balance is typically a debit. Asset accounts (Cash, Accounts Receivable) are debit accounts. Liability accounts (Accounts Payable, Notes Payable) usually carry a credit balance. Income carries a credit balance while expenses carry a debit balance. Everything else within double-entry bookkeeping is based on the above rules.

If, at the end of the month, the debits don't equal the credits, check for debits erroneously posted as credits, credits erroneously posted as debits, transposition of numbers (123 to 132), and incorrect math.

Here are some examples of common double entries:
- Cash income = debit Cash and credit Income
- Credit or accrued income = debit Accounts Receivable and credit Income
- Cash expense = debit Expense Account and credit Cash
- Credit or accrued expense = debit Expense Account and credit Accounts Payable
- Prepaid expense = debit Prepaid Expenses and credit Cash.

Assets, Liabilities, and Net Worth

Assets include not only cash, inventory, land, building, equipment, furniture, and the like, but also money due from individuals or other businesses (known as Accounts or Notes Receivable).

Liabilities are funds acquired for a business through loans or the sale of property or services to the business on credit. Creditors do not acquire ownership in your business, but promissory notes to be paid at a designated future date (known as Accounts or Notes Payable).

Net worth (or shareholders' equity or capital) is money put into a business by its owners or left in it as retained earnings for use by the business in acquiring assets.

The formula for this structure is:

$$Assets = Liabilities + Net\ Worth$$

That is, the total funds invested in assets of the business is equal to the funds supplied to the business by its creditors plus the funds supplied to the business by its owners. If a business owes more money to creditors than it possesses in value of assets owned and retained earnings, the net worth or owner's equity of the business will be a negative number.

This accounting formula can also be expressed as:

$$\text{Assets} - \text{Liabilities} = \text{Net Worth}$$

Cash or Accrual?

Many small businesses are operated primarily on a *cash basis*. The client buys products with cash and the merchant buys inventory with cash or short-term credit. As businesses become larger and more complicated, many keep records on the accrual basis. The dividing line between cash basis and accrual basis might depend on whether or not credit is given to clients as well as the amount of inventory required.

Accrual basis is a method of recording income and expenses in which each item is reported as earned or incurred, without regard as to when actual payments are received or made. Charge sales are credited at once to Sales and charged to Accounts Receivable. When the bills are collected, the credit is to Accounts Receivable.

Accruals should also be made for larger expense items payable in the future, such as annual or semi-annual interest on loans.

If you're comfortable with accounting, accrual can be the most accurate basis for records. But the cash basis is easiest to understand. As long as you don't prepay many of your expenses and are not incorporated, a cash basis is fine for your new consulting business.

Managing Accounts Receivable

Income not paid to you is called *Accounts Receivable.* Here are a few rules that can help you keep Accounts Receivable current. First, be sure bills are prepared immediately after the service is performed and the statement is mailed to the correct person and address and contains sufficient information to fully identify the source and purpose of the charge. Note that some businesses will simply set aside any bills that they question.

At the end of each month, age your Accounts Receivable. That is, list accounts and enter the amounts that are current, unpaid for 30 days, and those more than 60 days old. In fact, most Accounts Receivable computer programs will produce reports on aged receivables. Then call each account in the 60 plus days column and find out why the bill is unpaid. Keep an especially close watch on larger accounts.

To ensure that you get paid promptly, pay close attention to clients' complaints about bills. If a complaint is justified, offer an adjustment and reach an agreement with the client. Then get a date from the client as to when you can expect to receive the payment.

Managing Payroll Records

Quarterly and yearly reports of individual payroll payments must be made to federal and, in many cases, state governments. Each individual employee must receive a W-2 form by January 31 showing total withholding payments made for the employee during the previous year.

A payroll summary should be made each payday showing the employee names, employee numbers, rates of pay, hours worked, overtime hours, total pay, and amount of deductions for FICA (social security insurance), Medicare insurance, state and federal withholding taxes, deductions for insurance, pension, savings, and child support, as required.

To ensure that you maintain adequate records for this task, keep an employee card for each employee of your firm. The employee card or computer file should show the full legal name, social security insurance number, address, telephone number, name of next of kin and their address, marital status, number of exemptions claimed, and current rate of pay. A federal W-4 form completed and signed by the employee should also be attached to the employee card or record.

Also maintain a running total of earnings, pay, and deductions for each individual employee.

In addition, if your business employs union members, you may have additional deductions for union dues, pensions, and other fees.

To begin your payroll system, contact the Internal Revenue Service (Washington, DC 20224) and request the Employer's Tax Guide (Circular E) and get a nine-digit Employer Identification Number. The IRS will then send you deposit slips (Form 8109) with your new ID number printed on them. Use these deposit slips each time you pay your payroll taxes. Payroll taxes are paid within a month of the ending of a quarter; that is, January 31, April 30, July 31, and October 31. As your business grows, you may be required to pay payroll taxes more frequently. By then, your accountant will help you determine your needs and help in the process.

Managing Petty Cash

Most business expenses will be paid by business check, credit card, or placed on account with the seller. However, there may be some small expenses that will be paid by an employee or with cash that requires reimbursement. Because the amount is typically small, the fund from which the reimbursement comes is usually known as *petty cash.*

A petty cash fund should be set up to be used for payments of small amounts not covered by invoices. A check should be drawn for, say, $100. The check is cashed and the fund placed in a box or drawer. When small cash payments are made for such items as postage, shipping, or supplies, the items are listed on a printed form or even a slip of paper. When the fund is nearly exhausted, the items are summarized and a check drawn to cover the exact amount spent. The check is cashed and the fund replenished. At all times, the cash in the drawer plus the listed expenditures should equal the established amount of the petty cash fund.

Equipment Records

Keep an accurate and up-to-date list of permanent equipment used in your consulting services business. Especially, keep track of equipment useful for a year or longer and of appreciable value. Equipment records should show date purchased, name of seller, description of item, check number of payment(s), and amount of purchase including tax. If you own a number of items, keep a separate list for vehicles, computers and printers, and office furniture and fixtures. From these records you will develop a depreciation worksheet and provide supporting information for fixed asset accounts.

A charge to expenses should be made to cover depreciation of fixed assets other than land. Fixed assets are any item you purchase to use in your business for a year or longer. Examples are buildings, vehicles, equipment, furniture, and office fixtures. Smaller businesses will usually charge depreciation at the end of their fiscal year, but if your business grows and you have major fixed assets, you or your accountant may decide to calculate depreciation monthly.

As clarification, a calendar year is 12 consecutive months beginning January 1 and ending December 31. A fiscal year is 12 consecutive months ending on the last day of any month other than December. A short tax year is less than 12 months because your firm was not in business a full year or you have changed your tax year.

How to Price Your Consulting Services

You might think that this question—how much should I charge?—is one of the most important questions of the book. It really isn't. Many other questions will be just as important to the success of your business. However, this question is often the first one that new consulting services ask. So let's get it answered, first by considering the three Cs of pricing:

- Cost
- Competition
- Client

How much does my service cost me to furnish? Once you've established your start-up costs and your monthly operating costs, you'll have a good idea of how much your service will cost you to furnish to your clients. But there's one more important factor that you need: your amount of available time.

A month with 20 work days offers you approximately 160 hours of your time that you can sell to clients. You may wind up working more, but 160 is probably all you'll be able to bill to clients. In fact, depending on the size and structure of your business, you may not be able to bill that many.

Business consultants typically require about a quarter of their time to market their services and another quarter to keep themselves informed on the latest information in their field (read magazines and books, attend seminars, interview leaders). So they're down to 80 billable hours per month, unless they continue working after normal hours. If the operating or overhead costs calculated earlier total $6,000 a month, that amount is divided by 80 billable hours to come up with an hourly fee of $75. Depending on their specialty, demand for their service, and other factors, business consultants charge $50 to $150 or more per hour. Business consultants who work on larger projects often establish a per-diem fee that covers their costs for a seven-hour to ten-hour day.

Consumer consultants often spend less time marketing and learning than business consultants. Many consumer consultants can bill up to three-quarters of their time, about 120 hours a month. If the operating or overhead costs total $6,000 a month, that amount is divided by 120 billable hours to come up with an hourly fee of $50. Depending on what they do and for whom they do it, consumer consultants charge between $35 and $90 an hour. However, because the public prefers to pay for products rather than time, consumer consultants will set product prices based on an undisclosed hourly rate. A career consultant, for example, will offer a career placement package for $295 that is based on five hours of counseling and about $45 worth of materials.

How much are your competitors charging? A few telephone calls should get you the rates charged by your competitors. Of course, you must make sure that you're comparing apples with apples. Your competitor may not have your level of skill in this area, or may perhaps have more. Or your competitor may be including costs for some specialized equipment that you don't have. To determine your competitor's hourly rate rather than product price, ask them "If I preferred to pay you by the hour, how much would you charge?"

How can you find your competitors? Find a copy of *Consultants and Consulting Organizations Directory* edited by Paul Wasserman and Janice McLean (Gale Research, 1994) at larger public, college or business school libraries. It lists more than 5,000 consultants by name, location, services and other factors.

Why should you care what your competitors charge? Because your clients will probably get bids from them also.

You don't necessarily have to match or beat their bids, but you do need to know what their rates are so that you can help the client make a fair comparison.

How much do the clients expect to pay? Remember that the question isn't how much will clients pay, it's how much do they expect to pay? The difference is expectations. You may get some clients for your service to pay an excessive fee for a while, but they'll soon move to other sources. What you want to find out is what they think your service is actually worth to them. Most understand that, if they pay you too little, you will soon be out of business and won't be able to help them in the future. They may not admit to it, but they know it.

How can you know how much the client expects to pay for your skills? Ask a few of them. They may tell you what they're used to paying, what they think is a fair price, or maybe what they wish they were paying. Take them all into consideration. Ask the question of them and let them take a few minutes to explain why they think so. You'll get some valuable insight into what clients expect from you as well as what you should expect from them.

As before, make sure that you're comparing similar skills and similar fees. A client may expect more skills than you can offer—or maybe fewer.

Price vs. Value

Now you know what your time costs you, what your competitors charge for their time and skills, as well as what clients expect to pay for your service. So which figure is right? All and none. What you want is a price that will drive away about 10 percent of your prospects as too high and another 10 percent as too low.

Here's a technique that will make your business more profitable, put your business above your competitors, and keep your clients happy: sell value not price. How can a fancy restaurant charge five times as much as the diner next door for the exact same ingredients? They sell value. Call it ambiance or image or snobbery or nonprice considerations or whatever. The fancy restaurant makes the client's purchase an event rather than just a transaction. The fancy restaurant treats the client like a person rather than a number, gives extra service, uses finer dinnerware, and decorates the food to look more appetizing.

You'll see the same technique, selling value rather than price, in any competitive business where one firm wants to stand out above the others. Chevys are sold on price, Cadillacs are sold on value—and both are built by General Motors. Value says that, whether the price is large or small, you will get your money's worth.

So how does a consultant sell value? By establishing pricing based on results rather than time worked. For example, a marketing consultant may charge a percentage of the client's marketing budget to review, manage and audit it. A financial consultant could charge a percentage of return on investments rather than an hourly fee. Attorneys often base their fees in civil cases on a percentage of recovery. They may earn 25, 35, or even 50 percent of the recovery—or nothing, if they lose. Depending on your specialization, consider setting your fees based on value. This is an effective way of countering competitors who want to compare hourly rates.

Imagine seeing on the grocer's shelf a can of tomato sauce that was discolored and dented, the label torn. You'd probably pass it by for one that looked neat, fresh, and undamaged. Yet the contents of each can may be of exactly the same quality. Appearance does make a difference, especially in the consulting services business. For just a few dollars more, your business can develop a clean, professional appearance that will tell prospects and clients that you offer quality. Keep your office neat and orderly. Dress professionally. Use quality papers.

Price is the cost of something. Value is the worth of something. Why is your service worth something?

- You're knowledgeable; you know about consulting services and how to perform a valuable service.
- You're efficient; you know how to work smart to get the job done in less time.
- You're honest; you will not knowingly mislead your client or charge for services not performed.
- You're helpful; you want to solve the client's problem not just perform a job.
- You're fair; you charge a reasonable fee for an important service.
- You're accessible; you respond to questions, you answer telephone calls, you follow up with clients.

Successful consulting services don't shun the question of pricing or apologize for high rates. They look forward to the question so that they can explain why their service is worth more than that of other consultant. They sell—and deliver—value.

Establishing Your Consulting Service Rate Sheet

How can you develop a price list that is both profitable and competitive? By knowing what it costs to develop your service as well as how much your competitors charge for a similar service.

For example, you may determine that your primary service, time management consulting, requires that you charge $82 an hour for your services. You find that your competitors are charging $70 an hour for the same service. What should you do?

If you want to undercut your competitor (and maybe start a price war), you can price the service at $65 and make a smaller profit. Or you can offer it at the same price as your competitor and offer something your competition doesn't offer, such as a free time management system. Or you can compete by offering more individualized service, giving the perception of greater value. Clients want value.

A retainer is a contract that says you will be available to a client for a specific number of consulting hours (or services) for a set fee, and will not consult for the client's competitor. Retainers are popular with business and professional services, but are catching on with consumer consultants as well. Retainers offer security to both the client and the consultant.

How to Write Proposals and Contracts

A proposal is an offer to work with a client under specific terms and conditions. A proposal does not become a contract until both parties agree and either sign the proposal or sign a full contract written to expand on the proposal's terms.

Figure 5.3, on page 109, is a typical proposal for a business consultant. A proposal for a consumer consultant is much simpler, often in letter form.

You don't have to be an attorney to write a binding contract.

A contract must identify the parties involved, define the agreement of what is to be done, details of payment, and be signed by all parties.

Computer software is available that includes a variety of contracts and proposals. They include Legal LetterWorks (Round Lake Publishing; 203-438-5255) and 201 Legal Forms and Agreements (E-Z Legal Software; 305-480-8933).

AAA Management Services

Building Businesses for Success
935 View Street
Yourtown, CA 98765-4321
(567) 890-1234

Proposal for Consulting Services

On May 15, 1995, discussions were held between Bob Smith, owner of AAA Management Services and Mary Johnson, owner of Johnson Studios, for the purpose of enhancing Johnson Studios' profitability in the coming year.

In response to these discussions, AAA Management Services proposes to assist Mary Johnson and other owners and employees of Johnson Studios in producing and analyzing accounting records, making recommendations on increasing business profitability.

AAA Management Services' fee will be based on the number of actual hours incurred on Johnson Studios' behalf at the rate of $110 per hour. AAA Management Service agrees to submit weekly time reports every Monday for actual hours incurred during the previous week. Johnson Studios agrees to pay the invoices on presentation. Either party may cancel this agreement with seven (7) days written notice to the other party.

Johnson Studios further agrees to pay all authorized expenses when due.

For AAA Management Services   For Johnson Studios

_____   _____

Date:_____   Date:_____

Figure 5.3: Sample consulting proposal.

How to Work By Priority

Whether your clients know it or not, you are being paid based on the time you spend helping them. And you're being paid well for that time. Therefore, you must work by priority: most important tasks before least important tasks. By breaking down your job into specific tasks and scheduling each one, you can help ensure that all tasks are completed on time.

You can also prioritize your jobs into most important, less important, and least important to make sure that you're always doing what's most valuable to your business. A most important job is one with the shortest deadline, the quickest payout, the most important client, the greatest opportunity for your consulting services firm.

Of course, this doesn't mean that any of your clients are less important than any other. All have equal potential for helping your business succeed either through jobs they hire you to complete or through other clients they bring you. But the full-fee client who must have a special report for their Tuesday staff meeting has a greater need for your services than does the client who wants to start planning next year's strategy. So you prioritize your work based on the client's need as well as your own.

Where many successful consulting services can reduce costs through scheduling is by managing each job to balance both the client's need and their own. How do they do so?

If possible, group similar jobs together during the same time period, such as initial inteviews, to reduce preparation time. And, as available, give highest priority to jobs that provide your business with the greatest cash flow (cash, net 15 days, etc.) rather than slow-pay jobs (writing an article on local employment opportunities for a monthly business magazine).

A monthly planner can help with long-term planning and help you develop your daily planner or list of things to do.

How to Hire Good Employees

The best way to hire the right person for the job is to clearly define what skills are needed. Once you know what it takes to do the job, you can match the applicant's skills and experience to the job's requirements. This step will probably be easy for you if you're hiring an associate, but how about office help or other support functions?

Once you have a job description on paper, decide what skills the person must have to fill the job. Then, estimate the value of this service to your business. Finally, determine how much other employers in your area are paying for these skills.

When you know the kinds of skills you need in your new employee and their market value, you're ready to contact sources that can help you recruit job applicants.

Each state has an employment service (Department of Employment, Unemployment Bureau, or Employment Security Agency). All are affiliated with the United States Employment Service, and local offices are ready to help businesses with their hiring problems. The state employment service will screen applicants for you by giving aptitude tests (if any are available for the skills you need). Passing scores indicate the applicant's ability to learn the work, so be as specific as you can about the skills you want.

Private employment agencies will also help in recruitment. However, the employee or the employer must pay a fee to the private agency for its services. This fee can be from a month's to as much as a year's salary.

Newspaper advertisements are another source of applicants. You reach a large group of job seekers, and if you use a blind box address, you can screen them at your convenience. If you list an office phone number, you may end up on the phone with an applicant instead of with a client.

Job applicants are readily available from local schools. The local high school may have a distributive or cooperative education department where the students work in your office part time while taking trade or business courses at school. Many part-time students continue with their employer after they finish school. Consider local and regional business schools as well. The students are often more mature and more motivated than high school students.

You may also find job applicants by contacting friends, neighbors, clients, suppliers, current employees, local associations, service clubs, or even a nearby armed forces base where people are leaving the service. However, don't overlook the problems of such recruiting. What happens to the goodwill of these sources if they recommend a friend whom you do not hire, or if you have to fire the person they recommend?

Your choice of recruitment method depends on what you're looking for, your location, and your method of managing your business. You have many sources available to you. A combination may serve your best needs. The important thing is to find the right applicant with the correct skills for the job you want to fill, whatever the source.

A good employee is one who is skilled, reliable, and trustworthy. You may be the best judge of the applicant's skills, but how do you test reliability? Fortunately, there are standardized tests you can administer to measure potential of substance abuse, courtesy, maturity, conscientiousness, trustworthiness, commitment, and attitudes toward safety. One such test is produced by Wonderlic Personnel Tests, Inc. (1509 N. Milwaukee Ave., Libertyville, IL 60048; 800-323-3742) and requires about 15 minutes to complete the 81 true/false statements. The test is available in paper and computerized versions and costs less than $12 each. Wonderlic also offers a Personnel Test that measures the applicant's ability to understand instructions, potential for learning a job quickly, ability to solve job related problems, and ability to work creatively. Such tests can help you profitably find and manage better employees.

Understanding and Paying Taxes

Like it or not, the government is your business partner. And, as your partner, they receive a portion of your profits—even before you do. However, government can also help you make a profit through the Small Business Administration, Department of Commerce, state corporate divisions, and numerous other business services.

The owner-manager of a small business plays two roles in managing taxes. In one role, you're a debtor. In the other, an agent or tax collector, whether you want to be or not.

As a debtor, you're liable for various taxes and you pay them as part of your business obligations. For example, each year, you owe federal income taxes, which you pay out of the earnings of your business. Other tax debts include state income taxes and real estate taxes.

As an agent, you collect various taxes and pass the funds on to the appropriate government agency. If you have employees, you deduct federal income, social security insurance, or FICA taxes, and, in some states, you collect state income taxes from the wages of your employees. If your state requires sales tax on your consulting services business, you will collect it from your clients.

If you are a proprietor, you pay your income tax as any other individual citizen. Your income, expenses, and profit or loss are calculated on Schedule C, which is filed with your annual Form 1040. A partnership files its own tax forms and passes the profits on to the partners for filing on their personal income tax forms. A corporation files on IRS Form 1120 or short form 1120A. Sub-chapter S corporations file on IRS Form 1120S. Self-employment tax—social security insurance for the self-employed—is reported on your IRS 1040 Form using Schedule SE.

Individual proprietors and partners are required by law to put the federal income tax and self-employment tax liability on a pay-as-you-go basis. That is, you file a Declaration of Estimated Tax

(Form 1040 ES) on or before April 15, then make payments on April 15, June 15, September 15, and January 15.

Income tax returns from a corporation are due on the 15th of the third month following the end of its taxable year, which may or may not coincide with the calendar year. To find out more about your tax obligations, contact your regional IRS office (or call 1-800-829-3676) for the following publications:

IRS Publications

- *Tax Guide for Small Business* (Publication 334)
- *Guide to Free Tax Services* (Publication 910)
- *Your Federal Income Tax* (Publication 17)
- *Employer's Tax Guide* (Circular E)
- *Taxpayers Starting a Business* (Publication 583)
- *Self-Employment Tax* (Publication 533)
- *Retirement Plans for the Self-Employed* (Publication 560)
- *Tax Withholding and Estimated Tax* (Publication 505)
- *Business Use of Your Home* (Publication 587)

In addition, there are a number of federal forms you'll need for good record keeping and accurate taxation:

- Application for Employer Identification Number (Form SS-4) if you have employees
- *Tax Calendars* (Publication 509)
- Employer's Annual Unemployment Tax Return (Form 940)
- Employer's Quarterly Federal Tax Return (Form 941)
- Employee's Withholding Allowance Certificate (W-4) for each employee
- Employer's Wage and Tax Statement (W-2) for each employee
- Reconciliation/Transmittal of Income and Tax Statements (W-3)
- Instructions for Forms 1120 and 1120A for corporate taxes

Action Guidelines

As you can see, there are many responsibilities to managing the day-to-day operation of your consulting service. They include controlling operating costs, keeping helpful records, producing quality consulting services and cover letters at fair prices, managing employees, and paying required taxes. Here are some things you can do today to apply what you've learned in this important chapter.

✔ Estimate your consulting service's operating costs.

✔ Develop an estimated operating budget for your consulting service including sales, costs, and profit.

✔ Design or select a simple record-keeping system, including journals and ledgers or accounting software.

✔ If you plan to hire employees, establish a payroll system.

✔ Set up equipment records and keep them off-site.

✔ Establish your business's hourly rate and develop your price list.

✔ List ways you can sell value over price.

✔ Develop your own process for producing effective consulting services.

✔ Establish a simple but usable time-management system.

✔ Call the IRS toll-free number to order appropriate booklets and forms.

MARKETING YOUR CONSULTING SERVICE

S tuart Chase said, "The best mental effort in the game of business is concentrated on the major problem of securing the consumer's dollar before the other fellow gets it." One way to secure consumer dollars is through marketing. What is your consulting service's market?

A market is simply the group of prospects who would most benefit from certain services. The market for your consulting service is made up of those who potentially could benefit from your service—a very broad definition that will apply to you and to your competitors. Defining *your* consulting service's market means determining the characteristics of those who would most benefit from your unique combination of knowledge, skills, and resources.

This chapter will help you define your market and help you efficiently reach it.

The Purpose of Marketing

To understand how you will market your consulting service, you must first understand what a consulting service is. Consulting is a business based on knowledge and relationships. Period. Without both elements, you don't have a business. Because there are dozens of types of consultants—and hundreds of potential markets—we will use broad examples. But you'll quickly get the idea and be able to apply it to your specialty.

For example, how would you define the market for a consultant who can only work evenings and weekends, but cannot have clients meet at his or her home? That's who you are to your prospects. A prospect for this service is someone who is currently working and cannot take time off work to come to an office. In fact, your not having a regular office can be turned into a marketing advantage as you offer the convenience of meeting them at their home for the consultation. By defining your unique benefits, you can best define your prospects or market.

Let's say that the best opportunity for you and your skills is to specialize in consulting people on defensive driving techniques. In this example, who are your prospects? Your prospects are those who have had tickets or driving accidents. So how do you find prospects? First, you go where they go. You can typically purchase a list from the state department of motor vehicles or other resources. You limit the list to the geographic area you want to serve. Then you write to these people, offering your services.

Obviously, how you approach your prospects as a consultant will be somewhat different. Yet the principles will be the same. You will first determine whether there is sufficient opportunity for you to build your business and whether potential competitors are already adequately serving this market. Then you will focus your attention and your marketing on those who can best use your services.

Who are your prospects? They are those who have been influenced by your advertising as well as those recommended to you by satisfied clients. They are former clients, newcomers to the area, clients who need immediate help, and your competitors' dissatisfied clients. They are people who have never before required help or advice as well as those who frequently use the services of a consultant or advisor.

Some start-up consulting services begin their businesses by serving clients who cannot be served by their current or former employer. By working with them, you reduce the amount of marketing you must do to develop clients. Most start-up consulting services then pay a marketing fee or a finder's fee to these sources. It's another reason to maintain a good relationship with all of your past and current employers.

Let's look more closely at specifics on how to develop a profitable market for your consulting service.

Marketing Your Services

Marketing is a science. It's not a perfect science where the answer to a question is always the same. It's a science based on data, information, knowledge, and wisdom. Data is easy to get and build into information. From this information comes knowledge and, eventually, wisdom. Wisdom is what makes your business profitable. Marketing builds your business.

The purpose of marketing is to get more clients. That's it. If you're new to business, the purpose is to get your first clients. If you've established a substantial business, the purpose is to keep those clients that you have.

There are dozens of ways that you can market your services to prospects and clients. They include the many forms of advertising, as well as literature, direct mail, and telephone marketing.

Who Are Your Clients?

Clients are vital to your business. That's obvious. The better quality of clients, the greater the success of your business.

There are two ways of defining prospective clients or prospects: demographics and psychographics.

Demographics is a study of statistics about people: where they live, how much they make, how they buy, their favorite brands. Retailers use census information to build demographics that help them in deciding where to build a store. Consulting services can use demographics, too. They can learn who would use their services and, then, where to find them.

As an example, a consultant specializing in hotel operations must know more than the fact that prospects are a member of a specific trade association. The consultant must also know when hotel management needs the most help and how they typically find it. This information is available from experience, from industry studies, and from other experts in the trade.

Psychographics is the study of why people buy. You would think that most people buy for logical reasons. However, even in the business world, people often buy for emotional reasons and justify their decision with logical reasons. Knowing why your clients buy will help you sell to them more effectively.

If you've built a solid reputation in your area as a consultant whose name means quality, you can sell that name. People want to go with a winner, so you will get some jobs just because people know you were involved. So learn what makes your clients buy and help them to buy from you.

Understanding your clients is so important that large corporations spend millions of dollars annually on market research. Although some formal research is important, a small business can usually avoid this expense. Typically, the owner or manager of a small consulting service knows the prospective clients personally. From this foundation, understanding your clients can be built by a systematic effort.

Understanding buyers starts with the realization that they purchase benefits rather than products or services. Consumers don't select toothpaste. Instead, some will pay for a decay preventive. Some seek pleasant taste. Others want bright teeth. Or perhaps any toothpaste at a bargain price will do.

Similarly, industrial purchasing agents are not really interested in drills. They want holes. They insist on quality appropriate for their purposes, reliable delivery, safe operation, and reasonable prices. Video games are fun. Cars are visible evidence of a person's wealth, lifestyle, or self-perceptions.

You must find out, from their point of view, what your clients are buying, and why. Understanding your clients enables you to profit by providing what buyers seek: satisfaction.

So, people don't buy consulting services. They purchase practical advice to solve specific problems. They want accurate information that they can use to make more money or have more fun. They want knowledge that they can use. They couldn't care less about buying consulting services! Put yourself in their shoes and determine what they want, why they buy, when they buy, and how and where they buy these benefits. Then you will understand how to reach them.

Where to Find Prospects for Your Consulting Service

A *prospect* is a prospective client, someone who could potentially use your service but hasn't done so yet. They may not have heard of your service, or they may not know enough about your service to determine its value, or they simply haven't been asked.

Who is a prospect for your consulting services? Of course, that depends on what service you perform for clients. If you're a consultant who specializes in selecting appropriate pets for clients, your prospects are people considering finding a new pet. To turn these prospects into clients you must first think like they think, only faster. As an example, consumers who are considering a new pet may read classified ads or visit pet shops. The consultant can place an advertisement under "Pets and Supplies" offering advice on pet selection. The consultant could also offer a fee for referrals from pet stores.

The U.S. Census Bureau is an excellent source of statistical data for market surveys. Based on the latest decade's census, the Bureau divides large cities into census tracts of about 5,000 residents within Standard Metropolitan Statistical Areas (SMSAs). Data on these tracts cover income, housing, and related information that can be valuable to you. Results of the 1990 census are now available. For this and other market information, contact the Office of Business Liaison, U.S. Department of Commerce, Washington, DC 20230. The Bureau of the Census offers business statistics, data, and special demographic studies among its services.

How should you keep track of your prospects? There are many ways, depending on how many prospects are and how you plan to market to them. Some consulting services business owners use 3 x 5 inch index cards available at any stationery store. A typical prospect card will include both basic information—name, owner, address, telephone number, business, etc.—as well as qualifying information and notes from prospective contacts.

If you're using a computer to automate your business records, there are contact management software programs that will help you keep track of prospects. They range in price from about $50 for a simple system to $500 or more for a specialized prospecting system that can even help you write personalized sales letters. As an example, a good contact management program will give you standard fields or areas where you can type the firm name, contact name(s), address, telephone and fax numbers, the names of mutual friends or associations, and information about contacts. Some programs can even serve as a simple order entry form. If you're making regular telephone calls to prospects, the program may help you schedule callbacks, maintain records of conversations, and help you write personalized proposals that can be quickly printed for mailing or even faxed to your prospect while they're still thinking about you.

Depending on the service you provide and its cost, you may want to establish a screening or qualifying process for prospects. You cannot afford to spend much time on the telephone with people who will never become clients. You can require a small initial consultation fee or have an associate screen prospects for you. One successful business consultant charges for initial consultation unless the prospect has been in business for at least a year and meets other basic criteria. Then the initial consultation is free.

How to Sell Your Consulting Services

The majority of your prospects will make first contact with you by telephone. They may have read your ad in the newspaper or phone book, or heard about you from a mutual acquaintance. In any case, it is vital that you make the most of this first contact, answering their questions while getting answers to your own questions about them.

The prospect wants to know:

- Why should I use your service?
- Are you qualified to offer me effective consulting services?
- Are your services of greater value than the price?
- Are you trustworthy?

You want to know:

- What's your name and how can I contact you?
- How did you hear about my service?
- What do you need to know to make a decision to hire me?

Learn all that you can from the prospect. It not only develops a bond, but also establishes that you are a good listener—an important characteristic for success. In addition, you'll learn who's hiring and who's laying off, which trades use consulting services and which don't, and many other important facts.

Advertising on a Budget

The purpose of advertising is to tell your potential clients how they will benefit from using your services. The best way to do so is to let your other clients tell your prospects about their success with your service. That's called word-of-mouth advertising and it's the most valuable type of advertising there is. Unfortunately, it is also the slowest to develop. Your first satisfied client may, in conversations, mention your good service once or twice a month. After hearing that a number of times and if they are looking for your service, a prospect may call you for your service. By that time you may be out of business due to lack of work.

Consulting services must advertise. How much should you spend on advertising? Successful consulting services typically spend about 5 percent of their estimated annual sales on advertising. This can be as low as 3 percent or as high as 7 percent. For example, a consulting service with estimated annual sales of $100,000 should spend between $3,000 and $7,000 a year on advertising and promotion. Services located in areas where competition is tough may spend as much as 10 percent on advertising.

Successful consulting service owners suggest that the

majority of an advertising budget should be spent during months when business is typically slower. Rather than an ad budget of $250 a month, slow months may require a budget of $400 or more, while busy months will have a budget of $100. Long-term advertising, such as the phone book's Yellow Pages, require monthly payments.

Advertising is based on impressions. Every time that your prospect sees or hears your name, you make what's called an impression. It may be something small like seeing the sign in front of your business or an ad in the local paper. Or it may be a listing in the Yellow Pages or a positive (or negative) comment made by a mutual acquaintance.

Each impression is cumulative. After numerous impressions, large and small, your prospect may bring your name into the possible source part of his or her brain. Then, when a legitimate need for your service arises, the prospect considers you as a supplier. Think about it. How many times did you see or hear about Honda or Mr. Coffee before you even considered trying their product? Probably dozens or even hundreds of impressions were made. And consider that any negative feelings about these products are also impressions.

The point is that you will need to positively impress your prospects many times and in many ways before they can be upgraded to a client.

Besides advertising, there are numerous ways you can make positive impressions on prospects. One successful time management consultant developed and presented a low-cost Saturday seminar on managing time for success. Admission was $25 at the door, which covered the room rent, coffee, donuts, and printed handouts offered to participants. Of course, the consultant offered additional services including copies of her book on time management.

In addition, consultants can speak to other groups on a variety of employment topics. Kiwanis, Rotary, Lions, and other service organizations are always looking for informative (and free) speakers. Just remember that it must be informative, not just an opportunity to sell. Also consider speaking to special-interest clubs within your field of experience. You will be building your credentials as an expert.

Make sure you have an effective brochure (Figure 6.1, on page 127) that you can give to people who want to know more about your service.

Many successful consulting services develop much of their business through referrals. That is, they sell their services to those who work with people looking for jobs: counselors, human resources departments, businesses, employment offices, and executive placement centers.

Of course, you can enhance word-of-mouth advertising by developing testimonials. That is, when you have a client who expresses satisfaction with your service, you ask the client to write you a testimonial letter. The letter, on business stationery, will describe how professional your service is and how well you respond to the needs of clients.

Unfortunately, only a small percentage of those who say they will write a testimonial letter will actually do so. But the problem isn't sincerity, it's time. Most clients just don't have the time to write such a letter. So some consulting services offer to write a draft of the letter themselves and send it to the client for approval and typing on their letterhead. A well-written testimonial from a well-respected person will be worth literally thousands of dollars in new business to you. You will copy it and include it in with your brochure, quote from it in advertisements, and pass it out to prospects. It will be your best form of advertising. Of course, make sure that you have a client's written permission to use any testimonials you quote in advertising.

To encourage satisfied clients and their testimonials, some consulting service establish and promote a policy of satisfaction guaranteed. The profits lost are usually replaced by the profits gained through this policy. It is a helpful persuasion tool when trying to close a sale.

Do You Have A Vision For Your Business ❓

Would Having
More Customers...

And More Sales
Help Your Vision?

If you're like most small business owners, you want your business to grow and become more profitable. This enables you to spend more time with your family, take nice vacations, buy a better home, and have a happier, secure life.

The barrier that stops many owners from achieving this dream is the growth part. They are unable to get enough new customers and new sales. This doesn't have to be the case. See inside.

Figure 6.1: Sample brochure cover for a successful small business consulting service.

Free Publicity

There are many effective ways that you can advertise your consulting services at little or no cost. Exactly which methods you use depends somewhat on your specialization.

Once you have your business card printed, carry a stack of them with you wherever you go. Pass them out to anyone who may be or know a prospect. As you stop for lunch, put your business card on the restaurant's bulletin board. Do the same if you stop at a local market for anything: put your card on their bulletin board. All it costs is the price of a business card. In fact, order separate business cards for your specialties.

Many consulting services overlook one of the best sources of free advertising—publicity. As you start your business, write a short article or press release and give copies to your local newspaper, radio stations, shoppers, and other media. Include in it information about your business such as names of owners, experience, affiliations, background, expertise, purpose of the business, location, target market, and contact name. If your market is across an industry rather than a geographic area, send this press release to magazines in that particular trade, called trade journals.

You can promote your business and get free advertising by offering to write a newspaper or trade journal column on your specialty in exchange for an ad in the publication. A memory development consultant can offer a column on how to use memory to get ahead. A shipping consultant can write a column in a trade journal that reaches those who use shipping services.

If you're personable and would be comfortable doing so, offer to host a radio call-in talk show on your specialty. Or you can become a regular guest on someone else's talk show. The publicity will make you a local celebrity as well as an authority in your specialty.

Cable TV also offers opportunities for consultant owners who want to creatively market themselves. Talk with your local cable operator about current and upcoming channels that may need your services.

Also consider establishing an award or scholarship at a local high school, trade school, or community college in your business's name. Not only will you be able to deduct the award as a legitimate business expense, you can also use the award to promote your business in the local media.

One more proven idea—seek awards. Join professional and business associations, entering all applicable business contests. If you win any of them, from first place to honorable mention, use the award as an opportunity to promote your business through local and national media.

Newspaper Advertising

The majority of homes in the U.S. and Canada receive a daily or weekly newspaper or a shopper. From the advertiser's point of view, newspaper advertising can be convenient because production changes, if necessary, can be made quickly and you can often insert a new advertisement on short notice, depending on the frequency of the publication. Another advantage is the large variety of ad sizes that newspaper advertising offers. The disadvantages to newspaper advertising include the cost of a large ad, which is required to stand out among other large ads; the short-life throw-away nature of a newspaper; and the poor printing quality of newspapers. If you do decide to advertise in newspapers, establish a consistent schedule rather than a hit-and-miss advertising program. Most important, ensure that the program is within your budget.

Some consumer consulting services advertise in the classified ad section of their local newspaper. Depending on the size of the community, the frequency of the paper, and the cost, an ad in the appropriate categories can be a valuable investment.

Find out where your competitors are advertising and develop a better ad. Business consultants should use their trade journals for advertisements to reach new prospects. Go where your prospects go.

If there is sufficient savings, sign a contract for a specific number of column inches of advertising each year rather than a standard size. By doing so you are earning a discount as well as allowing for business fluctuations. Reduce the size of your ad when business is good and increase it when you need more business. Some contracts will allow you to change your ad as much as once a week while still earning a substantial discount.

Yellow Pages Advertising

Many consulting services say that an ad in the Yellow Pages is one of their best sources of new business. In most locations, if you purchase a required business telephone line you will get a listing in one category of your local telephone book. In some areas, this is optional. The listing may be as simple as:

AAA Shipping Services, 123 Main St......555-1234

Or the firm name can be in capital letters such as:

AAA SHIPPING SERVICES
123 Main St..555-1234

Or you can include information on your specialty, and even an alternate telephone number like this:

AAA Shipping Services
Specializing in International Cargo
123 Main St...555-1234
If no answer...555-2345

Many businesses upgrade their listings with space ads. A space ad is simply an advertisement that takes up more space than a line or two and is usually surrounded by a box.

To determine the size and cost of an appropriate space ad, check your local and nearby telephone book's Yellow Pages under headings for "Consulting Services" and related topics. Look for ads from competitors. When a potential client looks in their Yellow Pages, which ads stand out best? Which have the greatest eye appeal? Which are easiest to read? Remember that you don't need the largest ad in the phone book; you need the one that's most cost-effective for you.

The last few pages in your Yellow Pages frequently have information on how to select a space ad. You'll see terminology like double half, double quarter, triple quarter and columns. It's actually quite easy to follow. Most larger telephone books have four vertical columns per page; community phone books in rural areas are half-size with only two columns per page. So a triple quarter is three columns wide and a quarter page long; a double half is two columns wide and a half page long.

At the end of the Yellow Pages, there will often be a toll-free telephone number for ordering a space ad or listing. Or you may find the number in the front of the phone book under "Business Telephone Service" or a similar title. Also ask about cost and availability of color in your ad. The firm that produces your telephone book will help you design and write your ad. Then they will supply a layout of the ad and a contract for you to sign. Most Yellow Pages listing or space ad contracts are for one year and can be paid in monthly installments.

Building Repeat Business

A repeat client is simply one who hires you for more than one job. If the client is satisfied and needs your services again, you have a good chance of getting a repeat client. You didn't have to go out and spend additional money on advertising or work extra hours to promote your business. Your quality of business promotes itself.

The best way to get repeat business is to ask for it. As you call up your clients to determine their satisfaction, also ask them:

- Do you have any other jobs coming up?
- Would you like us to bid on them?
- What services do you expect to need from us in the coming year?
- Are there any related services that we could implement for you in the future?

You can also build repeat business by continually trying to sell your services to them. It is more productive to get more business from current clients than to find new ones. Here's how some successful consulting services build repeat business:

- Write a monthly newsletter to all clients with new information on your area of expertise as well as a listing of other services you offer.
- Perform value-added services, like offering a free copy of a book, booklet or article you've written on your specialty.

Earning Referral Business

Earning referrals is one of the most powerful types of business promotion. A referral is simply having one of your satisfied clients sell your services to prospective buyers. The word of a trusted businessperson is much more believable to prospects than is the word of an unknown businessperson or salesperson.

So how do you get your clients to refer prospects to you? You ask them to do so. In fact, it should be an automatic question that you ask: Is there anyone you know who may also need our services? Ask it right after you close a sale, as you start a job, as you complete a job, and—especially—whenever anyone compliments an aspect of your work:

"I really appreciate the advice you gave me on reducing my taxes."

"I'm glad to hear that. Is there anyone you know who may also need my help?"

In addition, once your client has referred others to you, many feel a stronger obligation to continue to use your services. It will not only help you grow your business, but will also help you keep the clients that you have.

Another source for referrals is The Consulting Source, Inc. (38 Ives Rd., East Greenwich, RI 02818; 800-382-1998). Donna-Jean Rainville offers a consulting search and referral service to businesses needing a specific type of consultant. She researches and recommends consultants based on their qualifications and experience within a field. The service is typically free to the business client; the fee is paid by the consulting service.

Action Guidelines

Learning how to effectively market your consulting service can quickly separate you from your competition. There have been many proven marketing ideas offered in this chapter. To implement some of these ideas for your consulting business, take the following actions:

✔ Define your consulting service's market. Who are your prospects? Who needs and will buy your service?

✔ Start a database of prospective clients or referral sources.

✔ How and why do your prospective clients buy consulting services? What are their expectations?

✔ Learn what your prospects have in common with each other. Do they read a specific newspaper or are they members of particular groups?

✔ Establish a low-cost advertising campaign for reaching your prospective clients.

✔ Find clients who will write testimonial letters for you or allow you to write them on their behalf.

✔ Carry a stack of your business cards wherever you go and post them wherever you can.

✔ Develop a cost-effective Yellow Pages ad in conjunction with your telephone company's advertising department.

✔ Establish your own techniques for developing repeat and referral business as suggested in this chapter.

Chapter

7

MONEY AND YOUR CONSULTING SERVICE

Money certainly isn't *everything*. But it is a convenient way of keeping score. In most cases, you will be monetarily rewarded in relation to the service you provide to others. The more you help the more you earn. How much of that you keep depends on how well you manage your money.

The purpose of this chapter is to ensure that you gain and keep an appropriate amount of money for what you do. It covers profits, cash flow, credit, financing, and other money topics.

Understanding Profit and Loss

Winston Churchill started a rebuttal speech by saying, "The substance of the eminent Socialist gentleman's speech is that making a profit is a sin, but it is my belief that the real sin is taking a loss."

Profit is simply the amount of money you have left over once you've paid all of your expenses. If you have more expenses than income, you have a loss. Pretty simple.

Of course, there's much more to profit and loss than numbers on paper. Your business can actually show a profit on paper, yet not have any cash. In fact, many profitable businesses go out of business each year because of negative cash flow.

How can you keep the cash flowing in your consulting services business? By keeping good records, watching expenses, and tracking the flow of cash in and out of your business. Before we cover cash flow, let's see how successful consulting services set up and use an efficient money-tracking system.

Tracking Your Money

As the owner of a consulting services firm, you need accurate information on a regular basis to ensure that your business is running smoothly. As a single-person firm, you may have all the information you need in your head. But as your firm grows you will need some information daily, other information weekly, and still other data on a monthly basis. Let's take a look at what you will need and when.

In order to manage your consulting firm, you will want the following information on a daily basis:

- Cash on hand
- Bank balance
- Daily summary of sales and cash receipts
- Daily summary of monies paid out by cash or check
- Correction of any errors from previous reports

You can either prepare this information yourself, have an office employee prepare it for you, or rely on your accountant. While daily records will not show trends, they will help you get a feel for the level of business that you're doing. And you'll be able to spot problems before they become serious.

Once a week, you or someone in your employ should prepare a weekly report on your firm. While still not sufficient for long-term planning, weekly figures will help you make small corrections in the course your business is taking. Weekly, you'll want the following reports:

- Accounts Receivable Report listing accounts that require a call because they are more than 60 days past due
- Accounts Payable Report listing what your business owes, to whom, and if a discount is offered for early payment
- Payroll Report including information on each employee, the number of hours worked during the week, rate of pay, total wages, deductions, net pay, and related information
- Taxes and reports required to be sent to city, state, and federal governments

Your weekly reports should be prepared by the end of business each Friday so you can review them over the weekend or early Monday morning.

Once a month, you will want to review a number of pieces of information that have accumulated through your daily and weekly reports but were too small to analyze clearly. Now that they are part of a full month, information about cash flow, Accounts Receivable, and other parts of your business make more sense, and can be more easily acted upon. Here are some of the reports and information you will want to see every month:

- Monthly summary of daily cash receipts and deposits
- General ledger including all journal entries

- Income statement showing income for the prior month, expenses incurred in obtaining the income, overhead, and the profit or loss received
- Balance sheet showing the assets, liabilities, and capital or current worth of the business
- Check reconciliation showing which checks were deposited and which were applied by payees against your business checking account, and verifying that the cash balance is accurate
- Petty cash fund report to ensure that paid-out slips plus cash equals the beginning petty cash balance
- Tax payment report showing that all federal tax deposits, withheld income, and FICA, state and other taxes have been paid
- Aged Receivables Report showing the age and balance of each account (30, 60, 90 days past due)
- Summary of Schedule C entries

Let's cover three of the most important documents you'll review monthly: your income statement, your balance sheet, and your cash flow forecast.

Your Income Statement

An income statement (Figure 7.1, on page 139) is a tally of the income from sales and the expenses incurred to generate the sales. It is a good assessment tool because it shows the effect of your decisions on profits. It is a good planning tool because you can estimate the impact of decisions on profit before you make them.

Your income statement includes four kinds of information:

1. Sales information lists the total revenues generated by the sale of your service to clients

Income Statement

INCOME
Consulting Services	82,000.00
Income from speaking, writing	13,250.00
Gross Income	95,250.00

EXPENSES
Owner's Salary	48,000.00
Payroll	20,000.00
Payroll Taxes	4,100.00
Rent	9,000.00
Office Equipment and Supplies	3,500.00
Telephone and Utilities	2,800.00
Insurance	1,200.00
Miscellaneous	1,100.00
Total Expenses	89,700.00

NET PROFIT (before income taxes)	**5,550.00**

Figure 7.1: Typical income statement.

2. Direct Expenses include the cost of labor and materials to perform your service

3. Indirect Expenses are your costs even if your service is not sold, including salaries, rent, utilities, insurance, depreciation, office supplies, taxes, and professional fees

4. Profit is shown as pre-tax income (important to the IRS) and after-tax or net income (important to you and your loan officer)

Your Balance Sheet

A balance sheet (Figure 7.2, on page 140) is a summary of the status of your business—its assets, liabilities, and net worth—at an instant in time. By reviewing your balance sheet along with your income statement and your cash flow forecast, you will be able to make informed financial and business planning decisions.

```
                    Balance Sheet

ASSETS
Current Assets
    Cash                                          8,278.15
    Accounts Receivable                           6,511.19
        less allowance for doubtful accounts        651.12
    Inventory                                       819.20
    Prepaid Expenses                              1,160.00
Total Current Assets                             16,117.42
Fixed Assets
    Land                                                 0
    Building                                             0
        less allowance for depreciation                  0
Total Fixed Assets                                       0
TOTAL ASSETS                                     16,117.42

LIABILITIES AND EQUITY
Current Liabilities
    Accounts Payable                              4,191.00
    Owner's Equity                               11,926.42
TOTAL LIABILITIES AND EQUITY                     16,117.42
```

Figure 7.2: Typical balance sheet.

The balance sheet is drawn up using the totals from individual accounts kept in your general ledger. It shows what you have left when you pay all your creditors. Remember: *Assets less Liabilities equals Capital or Net Worth.* The assets and liabilities sections must balance—hence the name. It can be produced quarterly, semiannually, or at the end of each calendar or fiscal year. If your record keeping is manual you will be less likely to develop a frequently updated balance sheet. Many accounting software programs can give you a current balance sheet in just a couple of minutes.

While your accountant will be most helpful in drawing up your balance sheet, it is you who must understand it. Current Assets are anything of value you own such as cash, inventory, or property that the business owner can convert into cash within a year. Fixed Assets are things such as land and equipment. Liabilities are debts the business must pay. They may be current, such as amounts owed to suppliers or your accountant, or they may be long-term, such as a note owed to the bank. Capital, also called Equity or Net Worth, is the excess of your assets and retained earnings over the amount of your liabilities.

Your Cash Flow Forecast

Your business must have a healthy flow of working capital to survive. Cash flow is the amount of working capital available in your business at any given time. To keep tabs on cash flow, forecast the funds you expect to disburse and receive over a specific time. Then you can predict deficiencies or surplus in cash and decide how best to respond.

A cash flow forecast (Figure 7.3, on page 142) serves one other very useful purpose in addition to planning. As the actual information becomes available to you, compare it to the monthly cash flow estimates you previously made to see how accurately you are estimating. As you do this, you will be giving your self on-the-spot business training in making more accurate estimates and plans for the coming months. As your ability to estimate improves, your financial control of the business will increase.

Every time that you have to purchase on credit, you add interest costs to your business. If you had more cash you would be able to save more on interest expense. For this and other reasons, you can reduce your costs by increasing cash flow.

The cash flow forecast identifies when cash is expected to be received and when it must be spent to pay bills and debts. It shows how much cash will be needed to pay expenses and when it will be needed. The cash flow forecast enables you to plan for shortfalls in cash resources so short-term working capital loans—or a line of credit—may be arranged in advance. Also, if you have excess cash, it allows you to put this cash to productive use and earn a return. It allows you to schedule purchases and payments so you can borrow as little as possible.

AAA Consulting

Cash Flow Forecast

DATE: Apr 1 1995
FOR TIME PERIOD: Second Quarter
APPROVED BY:
PREPARED BY:

FOR INTERNAL USE ONLY

	Date: Apr 30 1995		Date: May 30 1995		Date: Jun 30 1995	
	ESTIMATE	ACTUAL	ESTIMATE	ACTUAL	ESTIMATE	ACTUAL
Opening Balance	11,234.00	10,934.00	11,531.00	11,731.00	12,225.00	12,334.00
Collections From Trade	5,280.00	4,921.00	5,667.00	5,822.00	5,950.00	5,123.00
Misc. Cash Receipts	1,258.00	1,715.00	1,520.00	1,433.00	1,620.00	1,559.00
TOTAL CASH AVAILABLE	$17,772.00	$17,570.00	$18,718.00	$18,986.00	$19,795.00	$19,016.00
DISBURSEMENTS						
Payroll	1,945.00	1,955.00	1,945.00	1,936.00	1,945.00	1,989.00
Trade Payables	2,111.00	1,945.00	2,200.00	2,111.00	2,300.00	1,980.00
Other	786.00	765.00	822.00	754.00	833.00	875.00
Capital Expenses	789.00	899.00	800.00	812.00	820.00	844.00
Income Tax	2,123.00	2,192.00	2,123.00	2,146.00	2,123.00	2,111.00
Bank Loan Payment	567.00	567.00	567.00	567.00	567.00	567.00
TOTAL DISBURSEMENTS	$8,321.00	$8,323.00	$8,457.00	$8,326.00	$8,588.00	$8,366.00
Ending Balance	$9,451.00	$9,247.00	$10,261.00	$10,660.00	$11,207.00	$10,650.00
Less Minimum Balance	$10,000.00	$10,000.00	$10,000.00	$10,000.00	$10,000.00	$10,000.00
CASH AVAILABLE	($549.00)	($753.00)	$261.00	$660.00	$1,207.00	$650.00

Figure 7.3: Typical cash flow forecast.

Because not all sales are cash sales, you must be able to forecast when Accounts Receivable will be cash in the bank as well as when regular and seasonal expenses must be paid.

The cash flow forecast may also be used as a budget, helping you increase your control of the business through comparing actual receipts and payments against forecasted amounts. This comparison helps you identify areas where you can manage your finances even better.

A cash flow forecast or budget can be prepared for any period of time. However, a one-year budget matching the fiscal year of your business is the most useful. Many successful consulting services prepare their cash flow forecasts on a monthly basis for the next year. It should be revised no less than quarterly to reflect actual performance in the previous three months of operations and verify projections.

All businesses, no matter how small or large, function on cash. Many businesses become insolvent because they don't have enough cash to meet their short-term obligations. Bills must be paid in cash, not potential profits. Sufficient cash is, therefore, one of the keys to maintaining a successful business.

Consulting services face a continual cycle of events that may increase or decrease the cash balance. Cash is decreased in the acquisition of equipment or supplies. It is reduced in paying off the amounts owed to suppliers (Accounts Payable). Services are sold and these sales generate money owed from clients (Accounts Receivable). When clients pay, Accounts Receivable is reduced and the Cash Account is increased. However, the cash flows are not necessarily related to the sales in that period because clients may pay in the next period.

Consulting services must continually be alert to changes in working capital accounts, the cause of these changes, and their implications for the financial health of the company. The change in the cash can be readily determined if you know net working capital and the changes in current liabilities and current assets other than cash.

Let:

    NWC = net working capital

    CA = change in current assets other than cash

    CL = change in current liabilities

    Cash = change in cash

    Net Working Capital is the difference between the change in current assets and current liabilities:

$$NWC = CA + Cash - CL$$
$$NWC = CA + Cash - CL$$

This relationship shows that if we know the net working capital (NWC), the change in current liabilities (CL), and the change in current assets less cash (CA – cash), we can calculate the change in cash. The change in cash is then added to the beginning balance of cash to determine the ending balance.

At any given level of sales, it's easier to forecast the required Accounts Payable and Receivables than net working capital. To forecast this net working capital account, you must trace the sources and application of funds. Sources of funds increase working capital. Applications of funds decrease working capital. The difference between the sources and applications of funds is the net working capital.

The following calculation is based on the fact that the balance sheet is indeed in balance. That is, the total assets equal total liabilities plus owner's equity.

Current Assets + Noncurrent Assets + Retained Earnings = Current Liabilities + Long-term Liabilities + Equity

Rearranging this equation:

Current Assets − Current Liabilities = Long-term Liabilities + Equity − Noncurrent Assets − Retained Earnings

Because the left side of the equation is working capital, the right side must also equal working capital. A change in either side affects the net working capital. If long-term liabilities and equity increase or noncurrent assets decrease, net working capital increases. This change would be a source of funds. If noncurrent assets increase or long-term liabilities and equity decrease, net working capital decreases. This change would be an application of funds.

Typical sources of funds or net working capital are funds provided by operations, disposal of fixed assets, issuance of stock, and borrowing from a long-term source. The typical applications of funds or net working capital are purchase of fixed assets, payment of dividends, retirement of long-term liabilities, and repurchase of equity.

How to Improve Cash Flow

As you can see, to grow your consulting services business you need cash. Once you've analyzed cash flow and determined that you need more of it, what can you do? Depending on the specific type of business you own, you can find increased cash in your Accounts Receivable and in your inventory.

Accounts Receivable represent the extension of credit to support sales. In your business, the types and terms of credit you grant are set by established competitive practices. As an investment, the Accounts Receivable should contribute to overall Return on Investment (ROI).

Excessive investment in Accounts Receivable can hurt ROI by tying up funds unnecessarily. One good way to judge the extent of Accounts Receivable is to compare your average collection period with that of rivals or the industry average. If your average collection period is much higher than your competitors' or the industry norm, your Accounts Receivable may be excessive.

If they are excessive, it may be that you're not keeping tight control of late payers. You can check this by developing an aging schedule. An aging schedule shows the distribution of Accounts Receivable with respect to being on time or late.

Failure to closely monitor late payments ties up investment and weakens profits. The more overdue accounts become, the greater is the danger that they will be uncollectable and will have to be written off against profits.

If the aging schedule does not reveal excessive late accounts, your average collection period may be out of line simply because your credit policy is more liberal than most. If so, it should translate into more competitive sales and greater profits. Otherwise, you should rethink your credit program.

Developing Your Business Credit

Credit is simply someone's faith that the client will keep a promise. You buy a computer system on credit, and the lender believes that you will pay back what you've borrowed. Or, in the case of secured loans, you have assets that can be sold to cover what you've borrowed. So how do you build credit? Easy. You borrow a small amount, pay it back, borrow a larger amount, pay it back, and so on.

A good way to start building your business credit is to use personal assets—signature, real estate equity—as collateral for your business. One enterprising consulting service owner simply applied for a credit card in his business name from the same company that sponsored his long-standing personal credit card. He asked for a small credit limit, used it and paid it off, then asked for an increased credit limit. Meantime, he used the credit card as a reference for a new account with a supplier. Other new business people use equity in their homes or investment land as collateral for credit with banks and suppliers.

Where and How to Get a Loan

A recent survey of small businesses reported that 23 percent had lines of credit, 7 percent had financial leases, 14 percent had mortgage loans, 12 percent had equipment loans, and 25 percent had vehicle loans. For larger firms, the percentages about double in each category.

The ability to get a loan when you need it is as necessary to the operation of your business as is the right equipment. Before a bank or any other lending agency will lend you money, the loan officer must feel satisfied with the answers to these five questions:

1. What sort of person are you, the prospective borrower? In most cases, the character of the borrower comes first. Next is your ability to manage your business.

2. What are you going to do with the money? The answer to this question will determine the type of loan and the duration.

3. When and how do you plan to pay it back? Your lender's judgment of your business ability and the type of loan will be a deciding factor in the answer to this question.

4. Is the cushion in the loan large enough? In other words, does the amount requested make suitable allowance for unexpected developments? The lender decides this question on the basis of your financial statement, which

sets forth the condition of your business, and on the collateral pledged.

5. What's the outlook for business in general and for your business in particular?

When you set out to borrow money for your firm, it is important to know the kind of money you need from a bank or other lending institution. Let's discuss loans and other types of credit. There are numerous types of loans available, all with their own unique name depending on the lender.

Signature Loan. A signature loan holds nothing in collateral except your promise to pay the lender back on terms with which you both agree. If your monetary needs are small, you only need the loan for a short time, your credit rating is excellent, and you're willing to pay a premium interest rate because you're not using physical collateral, a signature or character loan is an easy way to borrow money in a hurry.

Credit Cards. Many a small business has found at least some of its funding in the owner's personal credit card. Computers, printers, books, office supplies, office overhead, and other costs can be covered with your personal credit card. However, interest rates on credit cards are extremely high—sometimes double of what you might pay on a collateral loan. But credit cards can offer you quick cash when you need it. If this is an option for you, talk to your credit card representative about raising your credit limit. It will be much easier to do so while you're employed by someone else.

Line of Credit. A line of credit is similar to a loan except that you don't borrow it all at once. You get a credit limit, say $50,000, that you can tap anytime you need money for business purposes. The most common is the revolving line of credit that you can draw from when business is off and pay back when business is good, providing that you don't exceed your limit. A line of credit is an excellent way for a consulting service to work through the ups and downs of seasonal business. With some restrictions, a line of credit can be established using a portion of your home equity as collateral. Using a secured equity earns you a lower interest rate.

Cosigner Loan. A cosigner loan should be one of the most popular loans for small businesses, but many business people never consider it. Simply, you find a cosigner or a comaker with good credit or assets who will guarantee the loan with you. If you have a potential investor who believes in your business but doesn't want to put up the cash you need, ask him to cosign for a loan with you. Your chances of receiving the loan are much better. Some cosigners will require that you pay them a fee of 1 to 4 percent of the balance or a flat fee; others will do it out of friendship or the hope of future business from you. In any case, consider this as an excellent source of capital for your new consulting service.

Equipment Leases. If you're purchasing equipment, computers, or other assets for your business, the supplier may loan or lease the equipment to you. This often requires about 25 percent down so be ready to come up with some cash of your own.

Collateral Loan. A collateral loan is one in which some type of asset is put up as collateral; if you don't make payments you will lose the asset. So the lender wants to make sure that the value of the asset exceeds that of the loan, and will usually lend 50 to 75 percent of asset value. A new consulting service owner often does not have sufficient collateral—real estate or equipment—to secure a collateral loan unless an owner uses personal assets such as a home.

Passbook Loan. Sometimes you can get a loan by assigning a savings account to the bank. In such cases, the bank gets an assignment from you and keeps your passbook. If you assign an account in another bank as collateral, the lending bank asks the other bank to mark its records to show that the account is held as collateral.

Life Insurance Loan. Another kind of collateral is life insurance. Banks will lend up to the cash value of a life insurance policy. You have to assign the policy to the bank. If the policy is on the life of an executive of a small corporation, corporate resolutions must be made authorizing the assignment. Most insurance companies allow you to sign the policy back to the original beneficiary when the assignment to the bank ends. Some people like to use life insurance as collateral rather than borrow directly from insurance companies. One reason is that a bank loan is often more convenient to obtain and may often be obtained at a lower interest rate.

For more information on business credit, write to the Federal Trade Commission, Washington, DC 20580; Attn: Public Reference. Ask for their booklet *Getting Business Credit.* It's free.

Managing Interest Rates

Money is a commodity, bought and sold by lenders. Just like other products, you can often save money by shopping around. Here are some points to consider as you shop for money.

First, are there any loan fees or other charges required to set up or service the loan? Some lenders will require that a loan fee of 1 or 2 percent, or more, be paid in advance. Others will even roll the loan fee into the loan, so you actually pay interest upon interest. Others will deduct a monthly service fee from each payment as it is made. This arrangement is not necessarily bad; after all, the lender must make his profit from you in some manner. Just make sure that you understand what the actual cost of the loan is before you agree to it. You also need to know actual interest rates as you compare rates between lenders.

Second, consider whether your best option is fixed rate or variable rate interest. Fixed rate interest means that the interest rate charged by the lender is the same throughout the life of the loan. Variable rate interest can vary during the term of the loan based on some outside factor. This factor is usually the cost of the money to the lender. Most variable interest loans have caps, specifying a maximum amount the rate can rise, both annually and through the life of the loan. The difference between the lender's cost and what he charges you is called the spread. From that spread comes his sales costs, office overhead, salaries, and profit. The spread is also based on the amount of risk he is taking in loaning the money to you. Higher risk means a higher spread. There are numerous indexes used to establish the cost of money. Review all of the options with your lender, ask which one makes the most sense for your needs, and get a second opinion.

Keep in mind that variable rate interest reduces the amount of risk the lender is taking, especially on long-term loans. He is virtually assured that, unless the money market goes crazy and goes over the cap, he will get his margin of profit from every dollar you send him. Lower risk means lower rates. The point is that you shouldn't disqualify variable rate loans from consideration. In many cases, they cost less than fixed rate loans and many lenders are more willing to make them.

To make sure that you pay the best interest rate available, don't jump into the arms of the first loan offer that comes to you. Shop around and compare. You may eventually decide to take that first offer, but only because you've found nothing better.

But don't worry about getting the absolute lowest interest rate available. You may want to accept your regular lender's loan terms, even though it's a quarter of a percentage point higher, in order to maintain a mutually profitable relationship. That quarter point may only mean a few dollars to you and will reinforce your business relationship with your lender.

SBA Guaranteed Loans

Erskine Bowles, SBA administrator, is making sweeping changes to the Small Business Administration, increasing funds and reducing paperwork. As an associate administrator recently announced, "What we're trying to do is get capital into the hands of people who have been capital starved."

The volume of business loans guaranteed by the SBA has increased from $3 billion in 1989 to approximately $9 billion in 1995. According to the SBA, the average loan was for $250,626 over a term of 11.5 years. About one-fifth of these loans went to companies that were less than two years old. Also important is that paperwork requirements for SBA guaranteed loans has been cut from as many as 40 pages to just 6 pages for loans over $100,000 and a single page for loans under that amount. Here is a summary of current SBA loan opportunities:

SBA 7(a) Guaranteed Loans. Private lenders make SBA 7(a) Guaranteed Loans, which can be guaranteed up to 80 percent by the SBA. Most SBA loans are made under this guaranty program. The maximum guaranty of loans exceeding $155,000 is 85 percent. SBA has no minimum size loan amount and can guarantee up to $750,000 of a private sector loan. SBA provides special inducements to lenders providing guaranteed loans of $50,000 or less. The lender must be a financial institution who participates with the SBA. The small business submits a loan application to the lender. After the initial review, if the lender cannot provide the loan directly, it may request an SBA guaranty. The lender then forwards the application and its analysis to the local SBA office. If approved by the SBA, the loan is closed with the lender, which disburses the funds.

SBA Direct Loans. SBA Direct Loans of up to $150,000 are available only to applicants unable to secure an SBA-guaranteed loan. Direct loan funds are available only to certain types of borrowers, such as handicapped individuals, nonprofit sheltered workshops for disabled workers, Vietnam-era veterans, disabled veterans, businesses in high-unemployment areas and owned by low-income individuals, or for businesses located in low-income neighborhoods. The applicant must first seek financing from at least two banks in their area.

SBA Microloans. The newest SBA loan opportunity, microloans, is intended for smaller businesses who want to get started or grow and only need a few thousand dollars. There is $65 million in microloan money available to small businesses. The typical SBA microloan is for about $10,000, though the limit is $25,000 for worthwhile small business ventures. Contact your regional SBA office for additional information and requirements.

Loan Applications. If you're interested in applying for an SBA guaranteed or direct loan, call your regional office of the Small Business Administration. Even better, ask for the name of an SBA-certified lender in your area. The SBA loan program, notorious for its paperwork requirements, can be expedited by a lender that knows how to work within the system. You'll get your loan faster. In fact, those bankers that have preferred-lender status can handle your SBA loan without the SBA even being involved.

Offering Credit to Clients

Offering advice in which people must trust you requires that you trust them as well. This means extending credit to your clients. Some consultants require prepayment for the initial consultation or purchase, then place the client on a net 30 days credit policy. Figure 7.4, on page 155, offers a typical credit application.

Common terms of payment for consultants include:

- Payment on receipt of weekly, biweekly, or monthly invoice
- Advance payment of weekly or monthly retainer, offset against weekly or monthly invoices for actual time
- Advance payment equal to a percentage of total fixed fee
- Total fee payable on completion of job

Many offer payment by credit card. Using credit card services, such as Visa, MasterCard, American Express, and Discover, can transfer bad debt problems to others and increase cash flow for your business. However, there is an initial setup cost and ongoing service charges. The credit card service will charge you a service charge of between 2 and 5 percent on each transaction. Talk with your lender about offering your clients the option of paying for services with their credit card.

Improving Financial Planning

Financial planning affects how and on what terms you will be able to attract the funding you need to establish, maintain, and expand your business. Financial planning determines the human and physical resources you will be able to acquire to operate your business. It will be a major factor in whether or not you will be able to make your hard work profitable.

The balance sheet and the income statement are essential to your business, but they are only the starting point for successful financial management. The next step is called ratio analysis. Ratio analysis enables you to spot trends in a business and to compare its performance and condition with the average performance of similar businesses in the same industry. To do this, compare your ratios with the average of other consulting services

AAA Consulting

CREDIT APPLICATION

DATE:

BUSINESS INFORMATION	DESCRIPTION OF BUSINESS

BUSINESS INFORMATION

NAME OF BUSINESS

LEGAL (IF DIFFERENT)

ADDRESS

CITY

STATE | ZIP | PHONE

DESCRIPTION OF BUSINESS

NO. OF EMPLOYEES | CREDIT REQUESTED | TYPE OF BUSINESS

IN BUSINESS SINCE

BUSINESS STRUCTURE
☐ CORPORATION ☐ PARTNERSHIP ☐ PROPRIETORSHIP
☐ DIVISION/SUBSIDIARY
NAME OF PARENT COMPANY
HOW LONG IN BUSINESS

COMPANY PRINCIPALS RESPONSIBLE FOR BUSINESS TRANSACTIONS

NAME : | TITLE: | ADDRESS: | PHONE:

NAME: | TITLE: | ADDRESS: | PHONE:

NAME: | TITLE: | ADDRESS: | PHONE:

BANK REFERENCES

NAME OF BANK | NAME TO CONTACT

BRANCH | ADDRESS

CHECKING ACCOUNT NO. | TELEPHONE NUMBER

TRADE REFERENCES

FIRM NAME	CONTACT NAME	TELEPHONE NUMBER	ACCOUNT OPEN SINCE

CONFIRMATION OF INFORMATION ACCURACY AND RELEASE OF AUTHORITY TO VERIFY

I hereby certify that the information in this credit application is correct. The information included in this credit application is for use by he above firm in determining the amount and conditions of credit to be extended. I understand that this firm may also utilize the other sources of credit which it considers necessary in making this determination. Further I hereby authorize the bank and trade references listed in this credit application to release the information necessary to assist this firm in establishing a line of credit.

X
SIGNATURE | TITLE | DATE

POLICY STATEMENT: INITIAL ORDER FROM NEW ACCOUNTS WILL NOT BE PROCESSED UNLESS ACCOMPANIED BY THE ABOVE REQUESTED INFORMATION. TERMS: NET 30 DAYS FROM DATE OF INVOICE UNLESS OTHERWISE STATED.

Figure 7.4: Sample credit application.

as well as with your own ratios over several years. Ratio analysis can be the most important early warning indicator for solving business problems while they are still manageable.

One note before we get into ratios: members of trade associations often will share their balance sheet, income statement, and management ratios with other members through studies and reports published by the association. It's just one more good reason to join one of the local or national consulting services trade associations. These percentages can help you in determining whether your consulting services business is being operated as efficiently as other firms in your industry.

Important balance sheet ratios measure liquidity (a business's ability to pay its bills as they come due) and leverage (measuring the business's dependency on creditors for funding).

Liquidity ratios indicate the ease of turning assets into cash. They include the current ratio, quick ratio, and working capital.

Current Ratio. The current ratio is one of the best known measurements of financial strength. It is calculated as follows:

$$\text{Current Ratio} = \frac{\text{Total Current Assets}}{\text{Total Current Liabilities}}$$

The main question this ratio answers is: Does your business have enough current assets to meet the payment schedule of its current debts with a margin of safety?

Let's say that you or your lender decide that your current ratio is too low. What can you do about it?

- Pay some debts.
- Combine some of your short-term debts into a long-term debt.

- Convert fixed assets into current assets.
- Leave in earnings or put profits back into the business.
- Increase your current assets with new equity (bring more cash into the business).

Quick Ratio. The quick ratio is sometimes called the acid test ratio and is one of the best measurements of liquidity. It is calculated as follows:

$$\text{Quick Ratio} = \frac{\text{Cash + Securities + Receivables}}{\text{Total Current Liabilities}}$$

The quick ratio is a much more exacting measure than the current ratio. By excluding inventories (typically small in consulting services businesses), it concentrates on the really liquid assets with value that is fairly certain. It helps answer the question: If all sales revenues should disappear, could my business meet its current obligations with the readily convertible quick funds in hand?

Working Capital. Working capital is more a measure of cash flow than a ratio. The result of the following calculation must be a positive number:

$$\text{Working Capital} = \text{Total Current Assets} - \text{Total Current Liabilities}$$

Lenders look at net working capital over time to determine a company's ability to weather financial crises. Bank loans are often tied to minimum working capital requirements.

Action Guidelines

Money is the root of all ... *business!* It's not that business people are necessarily greedy. They just want some assurance that they will have enough money to continue their business--and their eating habits. Here are some proven ways you can make and keep money:

✔ Establish a simple system for keeping informed on the financial status of your business on a regular basis.

✔ Watch your balance sheet carefully and learn to apply ratios to ensure success.

✔ Keep a running cash flow forecast, no matter how simple, to ensure that money will continue to come in when you need it.

✔ Learn how to develop and use your net working capital rather than borrow from the bank.

✔ Keep your relationship with your banker open and friendly—just in case.

✔ Talk to your banker about becoming a credit card merchant.

GROWING YOUR CONSULTING SERVICE

Business is like riding a bicycle—either you keep moving or you fall down.

This final chapter offers a collection of ideas and techniques from successful consulting service owners and other business people on how to make your business grow. It tells you how to solve small problems before they become big ones, manage employees and temporary help, insure against potential losses for your business and your employees, manage risks and catastrophies, and keep an eye on the future.

Solving Common Consulting Service Problems

As the owner of your own consulting services business, you deal with problems on a daily basis. So learning how to effectively solve problems can dramatically affect the growth and success of your business. Most business owners solve problems by intuition. By learning the necessary skills, you will become more comfortable with solving problems and reduce the inherent stress of your job.

What is a problem? A problem is a situation that presents an obstacle to your desire to move ahead. Here are a few examples:

- A client threatens to sue you for the results of advice you gave.
- Your industry is declining rapidly because of a recent congressional enactment.
- A computer program doesn't function as it should.
- A part you need for your copy machine is unavailable.
- An employee is undermining your authority with clients.
- New business income is down.
- You're two payments behind on a lease, and they've threatened to repossess your computer.

Where do problems come from? Problems arise from every facet of human and mechanical functions as well as from nature. Some problems we cause ourselves (hiring an untrainable employee). Other problems are caused by forces beyond our control, such as a tornado. Problems are a natural, everyday occurrence of life. However, if mismanaged, they cause tension and frustration that only compounds the problem. Successful business people must learn how to deal with problems in a logical, rational fashion.

Steps to Solving Any Problem

The solutions to some problems, such as how to plan an extraordinarily heavy work load next week, are typically simple and will require only a few moments of contemplation and planning. However, some problems, such as how to increase income by $50,000 in the next six months, are more critical to your operation and will require more time and effort. In fact, for critical problems, you may want to set aside a full day for analyzing the problem and finding the best solutions.

Recognize the Problem. Before a problem can be solved, you must first recognize that it exists. Here is where your approach to problem solving is crucial. You should not allow the problem to intimidate you. Don't take it personally. Approach it rationally and remind yourself that every problem is solvable if it is tackled appropriately.

Fear of failure can block your ability to think clearly. You can overcome this natural fear if you

- follow a workable procedure for finding solutions,
- accept the fact that you can't foresee everything,
- assume that the solution you select is your best option at the time, and
- accept the possibility that things may change and your solution fail.

Define the Problem. Once you recognize that a problem exists, your next step is to identify or define the problem itself. You can do so by asking yourself such questions as:

- What exactly happened?
- What started the problem?
- Did something occur that wasn't supposed to?
- Did something break that was suppose to operate?
- Were there unexpected results?

Determine Type. Then ask questions that help you identify the nature of the problem:

- Is this a person, equipment, operational problem?
- What product or service does it involve?

- Is the problem tangible or intangible?
- Is the problem internal or external to the firm?

Evaluate Significance. How important is this problem to the scheme of things? Ask yourself:

- Is this problem disrupting operations?
- Is this problem hampering sales?
- Is this problem causing conflict among people?
- Is this problem affecting personnel and their productivity?
- Is this problem affecting business goals and, if so, which ones?
- Is this problem affecting clients, suppliers, independent contractors, or any other external people?

Estimate Frequency. Some problems are 100-year floods that don't occur often enough to warrant extensive attention. Ask these questions:

- Is it a problem that occurred in the past and the main concern is to make certain that it doesn't occur again?
- Is it a problem that currently exists and the main concern is to clear up the situation?
- Is it a problem that might occur in the future, and the basic concern is planning and taking action before the problem arises?

The answers to these questions will help you focus on the true problem. You can't effectively research the causes of a problem until you have a clear definition of what the problem is. Sometimes, managers spend many hours on what they perceive as the problem only to learn, after seeking the causes, that something else was really the problem.

Selecting the Best Solution

As you answer these questions, you can begin developing a list of possible solutions. Go through this list and cross out those that obviously won't work. These ideas aren't wasted because they affect those ideas that remain. In other words, the best ideas you select may be revised using ideas that won't work.

Break the remaining solution down into its positive effects and negative effects. To do this, some consulting business owners write each solution they are considering on a separate piece of paper. Below the solution, they draw a vertical line down the center of the sheet, labeling one column "Advantages" and the other column "Disadvantages." Finally, they analyze each facet of the solution and its effect on the problem, listing each of the advantages and disadvantages they can think of.

One way to help you think of the advantages and disadvantages is to role-play each solution. Call in a few of your employees and play out each solution. Ask them for their reactions. Based on what you observe and on their feedback, you will have a better idea of the advantages and disadvantages of each solution you're considering.

After you complete this process for each primary solution, select those solutions that have the most significant advantages. At this point, you should be considering only two or three.

In order to select the most appropriate solution from these, consider:

- Cost-effectiveness
- Time constraints
- Availability of manpower and materials
- Your own intuition

Before you actually implement the chosen solution, you should evaluate it further. Ask yourself:

- Are the objectives of the solution sound, clear, and simple?
- Will the solution achieve the objectives?
- What are the possibilities that it will fail and in what way?
- How can I reduce the possibility of failure?

Taking Action

Finding the solution doesn't mean that the problem is solved. Now you need to design a plan of action so that the solution gets carried out properly. Designing and implementing the plan of action is equally as important as finding the solution. The best solution can fail because it isn't well implemented.

Design a plan of action chart including all the details you need to consider to implement the plan and when each phase should happen. Keep in mind, though, that the best plans have setbacks for any number of reasons. A key person may be out for illness or a supplier may ship materials late or a change at the client's site may require that the timetable be changed.

As each phase of your plan of action is implemented, you should ask yourself whether your goals were achieved, how well they were achieved, and did it work smoothly. To check your own perceptions of the results, get as much feedback as possible from your managers and employees. What you may think is working may not be perceived the same way by those closer to the action. Always remember that clients and employees are your most valuable resources in successfully carrying out your solution.

Managing Employees for Efficiency and Profit

The majority of employees in the labor force are under a merit increase pay system, though most of their pay increases result from other factors. This approach involves periodic review and appraisal of employees' performance.

When designing the plan of action, consider:

- Who will be involved in the solution?
- How will they participate?
- Who will be affected by the solution?
- How will they be affected?
- What course of action will be taken?
- How should this course of action be presented to employees, clients, suppliers, and others?
- When will the action start and be completed?
- Where will this action happen?
- How will this action happen?
- What's needed to make it happen?

An effective employee appraisal plan improves two-way communications between the manager and the employee, relates pay to work performance and results, and helps employees understand job responsibilities and expectations and areas for improvement. An employee appraisal plan also provides a standardized approach to evaluating job performance.

Such a performance review helps not only the employee, but also the manager, who can gain insight into the organization. An open exchange between employee and manager can show the manager where improvements in equipment, procedures, or other factors might improve employee performance. Try to foster a climate in which employees can discuss progress and problems informally at any time throughout the year.

To get the best results, use a standardized written form for appraisals. An appraisal form should cover the results achieved, quality of performance, volume of work, effectiveness in working with others in the firm and with clients and suppliers, initiative, job knowledge, and dependability.

To keep your pay administration plan in tune with the times, you should review it at least annually. Make adjustments where necessary and don't forget to retrain supervisory personnel. This isn't the kind of plan that can be set up and then forgotten.

During your annual review, ask yourself if the plan is working for you. That's the most important question. Are you getting the kind of employees you want or are you just making do? What's the employee turnover rate? Do employees seem to care about the business? Most importantly, does your pay administration plan help you achieve the objectives of your business?

Employee Benefits

Employee benefits play an important role in the lives of employees and their families, and they have a significant financial impact on your business. Consulting services cannot be competitive employers if they don't develop a comprehensive benefit program. However, if not managed, an employee benefit program can quickly eat up a small firm's profits.

A comprehensive employee-benefits program can be broken down into four components: legally required benefits, health and welfare benefits, retirement benefits, and perquisites.

Legally required benefit plans are mandated by law and the systems necessary to administer such plans are well established. These plans include social security insurance (FICA), workers' compensation insurance, and unemployment compensation insurance (FUTA).

Health and welfare benefits and retirement benefits can be viewed as benefits provided to work in conjunction with statutory benefits to enhance employees' financial security. Health and welfare plans are perhaps the most visible of all the benefit program components. They include medical care, dental care, vision care, short-term disability, long-term disability, life insurance, accidental death and dismemberment insurance, dependent care, and legal assistance.

Retirement plans are established to help ensure that employees are able to maintain their accustomed standard of living upon retirement. Retirement-benefit plans basically fall into two categories: *defined contribution plans*, which provide employees with an account balance at retirement, and *defined benefit plans*, which provide employees with a projected amount of income at retirement.

Perquisite benefits, or perks, are any other benefits an employer promises, such as a company automobile or truck, professional association or club membership, paid tuition, sabbatical, extra vacation, expense account, credit cards, or financial counseling services.

Health and Welfare Plans

When purchasing a health and welfare plan, select an insurance professional whose clientele is made up primarily of small businesses. In fact, if you can find one in your area, select one that's used and recommended by other consultants. Your insurer needs to be aware of the special problems that face small businesses, especially in your trade. Generous plans that look attractive and logical today may become a financial burden for your growing company. Remember that it is much easier to add benefits than it is to take them away.

Medical plans are usually the greatest concern of employers and employees. There are essentially two kinds of traditional medical plans. Major medical plans cover 100 percent of hospital and inpatient surgical expense as well as a percentage (typically 80 percent) of all other covered expenses. Comprehensive medical plans cover a percentage (again, generally 80 percent) of all medical expenses.

In both types of plans, the employee is usually required to pay part of the premium, particularly for dependents, as well as a deductible. Deductibles often range from $100 to $200 for single coverage and from $200 to $1,000 per person for family coverage.

A comprehensive medical plan is typically less expensive because more of the cost is shifted to the employee. Any plan you design should include features for containing costs.

As an alternative to a traditional medical plan, an employer may contract with a Health Maintenance Organization (HMO) to provide employees with medical services. The main difference between a traditional medical plan and an HMO is that the traditional plan allows employees to choose their medical providers while HMOs often provide medical services at specified clinics or through preferred doctors and hospitals. HMOs trade this flexibility for lower costs that are often passed on to the employee through reduced or eliminated deductibles or lower rates.

Disability insurance is an important but often overlooked benefit in small businesses. Disability insurance prevents a drain of financial resources to support a principal in the event that he or she cannot continue working.

Group life insurance is a benefit employees have come to expect in many regions and trades. Such insurance is usually a multiple of an employee's salary. Be aware that an amount of insurance over a legally specified amount is subject to taxation as income to the employee.

Recent legislation provides that employers who maintain medical and dental plans must provide certain employees the opportunity to continue coverage if they otherwise become ineligible through employment termination or other causes. In addition, new rules state that if a firm's health and welfare plan discriminates in favor of key employees, the benefits to those employees are taxable as income. Talk to your plan administrator about current laws and requirements.

Retirement Benefit Plans

Retirement benefit plans are either *qualified* or *unqualified* plans. A plan is qualified if it has met certain standards mandated by law. It is beneficial to maintain a qualified retirement plan because contributions are currently deductible, benefits earned are not considered taxable income until received, and certain distributions are eligible for special tax treatment.

Of the various qualified plans, profit-sharing plans, 401(k) plans, and defined benefit plans are the most popular.

Profit-Sharing Plans. A profit-sharing plan is a defined contribution plan in which the sponsoring employer has agreed to contribute a discretionary or set amount to the plan. Any contributions made to the plan are generally prorated to each participant's plan account based on compensation. The sponsoring employer makes no promise as to the dollar amount a participant will receive at retirement. The focus in a profit-sharing plan, and in defined contribution plans, is on the contribution. What a participant receives at retirement is a direct function of the contributions. At retirement, profit-sharing plan participants receive an amount equal to the balance in their account. Profit-sharing plans are favored by employers because they allow employers the ability to retain discretion in determining the amount of the contribution made to the plan.

401(k) Plans. Another type of defined contribution plan is the 401(k). In a 401(k) plan, participants agree to defer a portion of their pretax salary as a contribution to the plan. In addition, the sponsoring employer may decide to match all or a portion of the participant deferrals. The employer may even decide to make a profit-sharing contribution to the plan. As described earlier, the focus is on the contribution to the plan. At retirement, participants will receive an amount equal to their account balance. Special nondiscrimination tests apply to 401(k) plans that may reduce the amount of deferrals highly compensated employees are allowed to make, somewhat complicating plan administration. The 401(k) plans are popular because they allow employees the ability to save for retirement with pretax dollars and they can be designed to be relatively inexpensive.

Defined Benefit Plans. In direct contrast to a defined contribution plan, a defined benefit plan promises participants a benefit specified by a formula in the plan. The focus of a defined-benefit plan is the retirement benefit provided instead of the contribution made. Plan sponsors must contribute to the actuarially determined amounts necessary to meet the dollar amounts promised to participants. Generally, benefits begin at retirement and are paid over the remainder of the employee's life, so a defined benefit plan guarantees a certain flow of income at retirement.

As a business owner, you can establish your own retirement plan, called a Self-Employed Pension (SEP) plan. Call the IRS for a booklet (*Self-Employment Pension Plans*, publication 560) on how to start and manage these plans.

Selecting the Right Plan

Designing and implementing an employee-benefit program can be a complicated process. Many small businesses contract with employee benefit consulting firms, insurance companies, specialized attorneys, or accounting firms to assist in this task. As you establish your program yourself or with a professional, ask yourself:

- What should the program accomplish in the long run?
- What's the maximum amount you can afford to spend on a program?
- Are you capable and knowledgeable in administering the program?
- What kind of program will best fit the needs of your employees?
- Should you involve your employees in the design and selection of the benefit program? If so, how much and at what stage?

Certain plans are more suitable for consulting services, based on the employer's financial situation and the demographics of the employee group. Employers who are not confident of their future income may not want to start a defined benefit plan that will require a specific level of contributions. However, if the employees are fairly young, a profit-sharing plan or 401(k) plan can result in a more significant and more appreciated benefit than a defined benefit plan. The 401(k) plans are very popular now that IRAs have been virtually eliminated. However, the nondiscrimination tests make it more difficult for small businesses to maintain 401(k) plans. If your work force is composed mainly of older employees, a defined benefit plan will be more beneficial to them but more expensive for you to maintain.

Remember that while a qualified plan has many positive aspects, the qualified retirement plan area is complicated and well monitored by the government. Make sure you have adequate counsel before you decide on the most appropriate plan for your business.

Hiring Temporary Help

How does your consulting business cope with unexpected personnel shortages? Many businesses are facing this question whether the cause is seasonal peaking, several employees on sick leave, or an unexpected increase in business. For some skills, many consulting services hire and use independent contractors. But for office work, a growing number hire help through temporary personnel services. In fact, many new consulting services will start up their business renting part-time temporary office personnel instead of hiring full-time employees.

Using a Temporary Personnel Service

A temporary personnel service, listed in your phone book's Yellow Pages under "Employment Contractors–Temporary Help," is not an employment agency. Like many service firms, it hires people as its own employees and assigns them to companies requesting assistance. This means that when you use a service, you're not hiring an employee; you're buying the use of their time. The temporary personnel firm is responsible for payroll, bookkeeping, tax deductions, workers' compensation insurance, fringe benefits, and all other similar costs connected with the employee. You're relieved of the burden of recruiting, interviewing, screening, and basic skill training.

Most national temporary personnel companies also offer performance guarantees and fidelity bonding at no added cost to their clients. Equally important, you're relieved of the need for government forms and for reporting withholding tax, social security insurance, and unemployment compensation insurance.

If you need temporary personnel for a period of six months or more, it's usually more cost-effective to hire a full time employee. Also, if the task requires skills or training beyond basic office skills, it may cost you less to pay overtime to an employee with those skills.

Using Independent Contractors

An independent contractor is a self-employed person who performs a service for you. Because an independent contractor is not an employee, you cannot dictate the hours in which the service is performed nor, in many cases, where it will be performed. The advantage of an independent contractor is that they are not on your payroll.

A contract with an independent contractor should state clearly that the person is an independent contractor and not an employee. Otherwise you may have to pay social security and other payroll taxes on their services to you.

Many consultants expand their services by using the services of other consultants on a contract basis. These collaborations can help a consultant reach a new market with additional services without the expenses of adding staff. If you do establish a collaboration, make sure there is an equitable sharing of revenue based on who found the client, who will do most of the work, and who brings more to the collaboration.

Using Temporary Employees Efficiently

The key to successful use of temporary employees is in planning what type of help you will need, how much, and when. The accurate information you give to the temporary service firm will improve their efficiency in supplying the correct person for your needs.

Before your temporary employee arrives on the job, there are a few things you should do. First, appoint one of your permanent employees to supervise the temporary employee and check on the progress of the work. Be sure this supervisor understands the job and its responsibilities. Next, let your permanent staff know that you're taking on extra help and that it will be temporary. Explain why the extra help is needed and ask them to cooperate with the new employee in any way possible.

Have everything ready before the temporary employee arrives. The work to be done should be organized and laid out so that the employee can begin producing with a minimum of time spent in adjusting to the job and the surroundings. Also, don't set up schedules that are impossible to complete within the time you allot. Try to stay within the time limits you gave the temporary help service but plan to extend the time period if necessary, rather than hurry the employee.

Finally, furnish detailed instructions. Describe your type of business and the services you offer. Help the temp feel comfortable and part of your team. Most temporary employees have broad business experience and can easily adapt to your requirements—if they know what they are.

Managing Risk

You've learned how to increase sales and reduce expenses for your consulting services business. But even as your business grows and profits, you can still lose money. How?

- An employee is injured on the job and sues you.
- An employee runs off with money stolen from your business.
- A fire or flood wipes out your office, equipment, and important records.

- A partner in your business files bankruptcy and the courts attach your business.
- The local economy goes sour and you can't find enough work for six months or more.
- A business partner is involved in a divorce settlement and business assets must be sold to meet a court order.
- The IRS comes after you for a large tax bill they think you owe them and takes over your bank account until everything is resolved.

The list goes on. There are many ways that an otherwise profitable business can quickly be thrown into a situation where the business's future is in jeopardy. What can you do about it? First, you can make sure you understand the risks involved in your business. And, second, you can take precautions to ensure that the risks are minimal. They will never go away, but, through smart risk management, you can minimize them and prepare for the worst.

Identifying Potential Risks

Of course, the best time to minimize the risk of business disasters is before they happen. And the first step to minimizing risk is identifying the risks that can occur. Business risks that consulting services typically face are:

- Acts of nature (fire, flood)
- Acts of man (theft, vandalism, vehicle accidents)
- Personal injury (employee or user)
- Legal problems (liens, unfair trade practices, torts)
- Financial (loss of income, funding, or assets)
- Taxation (judgments, tax liens)
- Management (loss of owner's capacity to manage or partner's ownership)

Of course, every method of reducing risk—attorneys, insurance, binding agreements, security systems, fire alarms—cost money. So when is it more cost-effective to accept the risk rather than pay for products or services that eliminate the risk? It's a simple question with a simple answer: it all depends.

Actually, the best time to minimize risk in your business is right now. The real answer lies in balancing the cost of loss against the cost of security. There are a number of ways that you can keep your losses to a minimum. They include preventing or limiting exposure to loss, risk retention, transferring risk, and insurance.

One principle of loss prevention and control is the same in business as it is in your personal life: avoid activities that are too hazardous. For example, don't leave cash or valuable equipment where it can be easily stolen.

A consulting service business owner may decide that the firm can afford to absorb some losses, either because the frequency and probability of loss are low or because the dollar value of loss is manageable. Maybe your consulting services business owns an older vehicle and their drivers have excellent safety records, so you decide to drop the collision insurance on these vehicles but retain it on newer vehicles.

Insuring Against Risks

The most common method of transferring risk is purchasing insurance. By insuring your business and equipment, you have transferred much of the risk of loss to the insurance company. You pay a relatively small amount in premium rather than run the risk of not protecting yourself against the possibility of a much larger financial loss.

Of course, you can be overinsured or pay more than is necessary for the amount of risk that you transfer. That's why it's so important to select a reputable and professional insurance agent to advise you. But in business insurance, only you can decide which exposures you absolutely must insure against. Some decisions, however, are already made for you: those required by law and those required by others as a part of doing business with them. Workers' compensation insurance is an example of insurance that is required by law. Your bank probably won't lend you money for equipment, real estate, or other assets unless you insure them against loss.

Today, very few businesses—and especially consulting services—have sufficient financial reserves to protect themselves against the hundreds of property and liability exposures that they face. What those exposures are, what their dollar value is, and how much is enough, are difficult questions. As you build a team of business professionals to help you effectively manage your business, you should use an insurance professional.

Four kinds of insurance are essential to your business: fire, liability, automobile, and workers' compensation insurance. Selecting from among the dozens of available policies and options can be somewhat confusing to most business people. However, the insurance information on pages 180–181 will guide you in making the right decisions for the right reasons.

Increasing Income

To grow your business you must increase the number of clients you serve or increase what you are charging the clients you have. Because there are just so many billable hours in a consultant's day, most established consultants opt to periodically increase fees.

The best way to do this is to gracefully give up the bottom ten percent of your clients each year in favor of finding ten percent more for which you can charge your new, higher fees. Rather than desert these clients, recommend a consultant in your field who charges less than you do. For this favor you can ask the consultant for a finder's fee or you can ask for referrals from them of large clients they may not feel comfortable serving.

Business Insurance Tips

Fire Insurance

- You can add other perils—such as windstorm, hail, smoke, explosion, vandalism, and malicious mischief—to your basic fire insurance at a relatively small additional fee.

- If you need comprehensive coverage, your best buy may be one of the all-risk contracts—such as the $1 million umbrella policy—that offers the broadest available protection for the money.

- Remember that the insurance company may compensate your losses by paying actual cash value of the property at the time of the loss, it may repair or replace the property with material of like kind and quality, or it may take all the property at the agreed or appraised value and reimburse you for your loss.

- Even if you have several policies on your property, you can still collect only the amount of your actual cash loss. All the insurers share the payment proportionately.

- Special protection other than the standard fire insurance policy is needed to cover the loss by fire of accounts, bills, currency, deeds, evidence of debt, and securities.

- After a loss, you must use all reasonable means to protect the property from further loss or run the risk of having your coverage canceled.

- In most cases, to recover your loss you must furnish within 60 days a complete inventory of the damaged, destroyed, and undamaged property showing in detail quantities, costs, actual cash value, and amount of loss claimed.

- If you and your insurer disagree on the amount of the loss, the question may be resolved through special appraisal procedures provided for in the fire insurance policy.

- You may cancel your policy without notice at any time and get part of the premium returned. The insurance company also may cancel at any time within a specified period, usually five days, with a written notice to you.

Liability Insurance

- You may be legally liable for damages even in cases where you used reasonable care.

- Under certain conditions, your business may be subject to damage claims even from trespassers.

- Most liability policies require you to notify the insurer immediately after an incident on your property that might cause a future claim. This holds true no matter how unimportant the incident may seem at the time it happens.

- Even if the suit against you is false or fraudulent, the liability insurer pays court costs, legal fees, and interest on judgments in addition to the liability judgments themselves.
- You can be liable for the acts of others under contracts you have signed with them, such as independent contractors. This liability is insurable.

Automobile Insurance

- When an employee uses a car on your behalf, you can be legally liable even though you don't own the car or truck.
- You can often get deductibles of almost any amount—$250, $500, $1,000—and thereby reduce your premiums.
- Automobile medical-payments insurance pays for medical claims, including your own, arising from vehicular accidents regardless of the question of negligence.
- In most states, you must carry liability insurance or be prepared to provide a surety bond or other proof of financial responsibility when you're involved in an accident.
- You can purchase uninsured motorist protection to cover your own bodily injury claims from someone who has no insurance.
- Personal property stored in a car or truck and not attached to it is not covered under an automobile policy.

Workers' Compensation Insurance

- Federal laws require that an employer provide employees a safe place to work, hire competent fellow employees, provide safe tools, and warn employees of existing danger. Whether or not an employer provides these things, he is liable for damage suits brought by an employee and possible fines or prosecution.
- State law determines the level or type of benefits payable under workers' compensation insurance policies.
- Not all employees are covered by workers' compensation insurance laws. The exceptions are determined by state law and therefore vary from state to state.
- You can save money on workers' compensation insurance by seeing that your employees are properly classified. Rates for workers' compensation insurance vary from 0.1 percent of the payroll for safe occupations to about 25 percent or more of the payroll for very hazardous occupations.
- Most employers can reduce their workers' compensation insurance premium cost by reducing their accident rates below the average. They do this by using safety and loss-prevention measures established by the individual state.

If you don't have extensive business experience—and even if you do—read Harold Wright's invaluable book *How to Make a 1,000 Mistakes in Business and Still Succeed* (The Wright Track, 1990). Hal points out which decisions are most important in the success of your business and how to make them correctly. It's also a very entertaining book.

Dealing with Business Cycles

No businesses are truly recession-proof. All businesses have cycles where sales become easier or harder to make. Consulting services are subject to the same business cycle that most businesses face. Even so, there are steps you can take to minimize the market's downswing and extend its upswing.

First, determine the business cycle for your industry or market. Reviewing income and financial records from prior years, or checking with the local chamber of commerce, you can draw a chart illustrating the local business cycle. In your region, it may be that most of the market for your service occurs in the spring and summer. Or maybe in the winter and fall. Or the cycle may be fairly equal across the year, but alternate years may fluctuate up or down. The first step to coping with recessions in the local business cycle is to determine exactly what and when that cycle is.

The next step is to begin planning for it. That is, if you're coming up to a typically slower period, determine what you need to do. In past years, how much has income dropped? For how long? Can you find income sources in other specialities where the cycle is moving up? What expenses can you cut? Do you have an employee who would like a seasonal layoff so he can catch up on other interests? Maybe you need to dramatically cut back on your expenses and debts for this period. If so, list them out now, determine which will naturally diminish and which will need to be reduced.

One successful consulting service owner, while in a busy period, decided that times would be much slower six months hence. So he talked with his bank and other creditors, offering to prepay debts and expenses now so he could reduce payments later. It worked. When times got rougher, he reduced his expenses and weathered the problem.

If you aren't into your slow season yet, you can also talk to your lender about building a line of credit now that will help you get through the tougher times ahead.

Another source for cash to tide you through a recession is available from a second mortgage on your building, your home, or other large asset. Speak with your lender about this opportunity. Even if you decide not to take out a second mortgage, you will be ready if and when you need to do so.

Consider widening your market. That is, travel to a nearby metropolitan area and study whether you can expand your services to reach it. If so, you can pick up additional sales by either subcontracting your services or by promoting your services in the expanded market. It certainly beats starving at home.

Advanced Expense Management for Consulting Services

Consultant and author Alan Weiss says, "It doesn't matter at all—not at all—what your billings are or how much you make. The only thing that matters is how much you keep."

Every dollar saved in overhead is a dollar on the bottom line of net profit—and a dollar less borrowed. The object of reducing costs in your consulting services business is to increase profits. Increasing profits through cost reduction must be based on the concept of an organized, planned program. Unless adequate records are maintained through an efficient and accurate accounting system, there can be no basis for analyzing costs.

Cost reduction is not simply attempting to slash any and all expenses without order. The owner-manager must understand the nature of expenses and how expenses interrelate with sales, inventories, overhead, gross profits, and net profits. Nor does cost reduction mean only the reduction of specific expenses. You can achieve greater profits through more efficient use of your expense dollar. Some of the ways you do this are by increasing the average sale per client, by getting a larger return for your promotion and sales dollar, and by improving your internal methods and procedures.

As an example, one telecommunications consultant was quite pleased when, in a single year, sales went from $40,000 to $200,000. However, at the end of the year, records showed that net profit the prior year, with lower sales, was actually higher. Why? Because the expenses of doing business grew at a rate faster than the income.

Your goal should be to pay the right price for prosperity. Determining that price for your operation goes beyond knowing what your expenses are. Reducing expenses to increase profit requires that you obtain the most efficient use of your expense dollars.

Checking job records, you might determine that one of your employees is significantly less efficient than other employees performing the same tasks. You can then reduce expenses by increasing this employee's efficiency through training. By watching this employee perform his or her job, you can determine where the inefficiencies are and help him or her to overcome them. If done with consideration for the person, he or she will appreciate your attention, and so will your profit line.

Sometimes you cannot cut an expense item. But you can get more from it and thus increase your profits. In analyzing your expenses you should use percentages rather than actual dollar amounts. For example, if you increase sales and keep the dollar amount of an expense the same, you have decreased that expense as a percentage of income. When you decrease your cost percentage, you increase your percentage of profit.

On the other hand, if your sales volume remains the same, you can increase the percentage of profit by reducing a specific item of expense. Your goal, of course, is to simultaneously decrease specific expenses and increase their productive worth.

Before you can determine whether cutting expenses will increase profits, you need information about your operation. This information can be obtained only if you adequately use record-keeping and financial management systems discussed earlier.

Locating Reducible Expenses

Your income statement provides a summary of expense information and is the focal point in locating expenses that can be cut. For this reason, the information should be as current as possible. As a report of what has already been spent, an income statement alerts you to expense items that should be watched in the present business period. If you get an income statement only at the end of the year, you should consider having one prepared more often. At the end of each quarter is usually sufficient for smaller firms. Larger consulting services should receive the information on a monthly basis.

Regardless of the frequency, the best option is to prepare two income statements. One statement should report the sales, expenses, profit and loss of your operations cumulatively for the current business year to date. The other statement should report on the same items for the last complete month or quarter. Each of the statements should also carry the following information:

- This year's figures and each item as a percentage of sales
- Last year's figures and the percentages

- The difference between last year and this year—over or under
- Budgeted figures and the respective percentages
- The difference between current year actuals and the budgeted figures—over or under
- Average percentages for similar businesses (available from trade associations and the U.S. Department of Labor)
- The difference between your annual percentages and the industry ratios—over or under

This information allows you to locate expense variations in three ways:

1. By comparing this year to last year.

2. By comparing expenses to your own budgeted figures.

3. By comparing your percentages to the operating ratios for similar businesses.

The important basis for comparison is the percentage figure. It represents a common denominator for all three methods. When you have indicated the percentage variations, you should then study the dollar amounts to determine what kind of corrective action is needed.

Because your cost cutting will come largely from variable expenses, you should make sure that they are indicated on your income statements. Variable expenses are those that fluctuate with the increase or decrease of sales volume. Some of them are overtime, temporary help, advertising, salaries, commissions, and payroll taxes. Fixed expenses are those that stay the same regardless of sales volume. Among them are your salary, salaries for permanent employees, depreciation, rent, and utilities.

When you have located a problem expense area, the next step obviously is to reduce that cost so as to increase your profit. A key to the effectiveness of your cost-cutting action is the worth of the various expenditures. As long as you know the worth of your expenditures, you can profit by making small improvements in expenses. Keep an open eye and an open mind. It is better to do a spot analysis once a month than to wait several months and then do a detailed study.

Take action as soon as possible. You can refine your cost-cutting action as you go along. Be persistent. Results typically come slower than you might like. Keep in mind that only persistent analysis of your records and constant action can help keep expenses from eating up profit.

Reducing Overhead

Business overhead is simply the cost of keeping your doors open. If your consulting services business is located in your home, overhead costs are probably small. But if you have a shop, an office, and office personnel, your overhead is greater. It's also large if you have high debt to banks, suppliers, and backers.

The suggestion made earlier in this book was to start out small and let your growing business force you into larger quarters. That is, depending on your consulting services market, start with an office in a corner of your home. Then, as business grows, take on greater obligations for additional overhead. If you build the client's perception of quality with your product, you won't have to maintain impressive offices. Few clients will decide not to do business with you because your office is in your home.

You can also reduce overhead by carefully watching the costs of supplies. Printed stationery is an excellent way to promote the quality of your business, but you don't need printed notepads unless the client will see them. For the price of generic ink pens you can often get ones that include your business name and phone number. But don't buy so many that they wind up costing more than quality ink pens because you've changed your address or phone number. Buy supplies in quantity if you can, but don't buy more than you will use in three to six months unless you're certain that they won't become out-of-date.

Travel expenses can easily get out of hand without good record keeping. That means developing a simple system for tracking transportation, lodging, meals, phone, and other costs. Figure 8.1, on page 189, is a typical travel expense report form.

Labor cost is one expense that can quickly eat away the profits of a small consulting services business. Don't hire an office manager or secretary until you absolutely must. It's more profitable to do the required filing and office functions yourself after normal business hours or on weekends. Or you can ask the help of a spouse or older child who could be put on the payroll as soon as your business can afford it.

Some small consulting services use temporary help or outside services rather than hire employees and deal with all the taxes and records that come with it. They have records kept by a bookkeeping or accounting service, office cleaning is done by a janitorial service (or the boss), telephones are answered by an answering service, correspondence and retyping service is performed by a secretarial service. Consulting services jobs that the owner can't handle are contracted out to other consultants. They know that the complexity of regulations and taxation is endlessly multiplied when the first employee is hired—so they avoid hiring anyone until their success requires them to do so.

Long-distance phone calls can quickly add to your expenses and cut into your profits, especially when they are personal calls made by employees. Many successful consulting services use a telephone call record to keep track of long-distance calls, then compare the report with the monthly phone bill. Calls not listed on the report are assumed to be personal calls and should be checked out.

AAA Consulting

EXPENSE REPORT

Attach Receipts

EXPENSE ACCOUNT OF: Bill Smith   For Period From: Jun 11 1995   To: Jun 17 1995

DATE	TRAVELLED FROM	TRAVELLED TO	MI/KM	TRANS-PORT.	HOTEL	MEALS BKFST.	MEALS LUNCH	MEALS DINNER	PHONE	PARKING	MISC. EXPLAIN BELOW *	DAILY TOTAL
SAT												
SUN	Yourtown	Theirtown	229		$58.60		$7.90	$11.40	$4.15			$82.05
MON	Convention				$58.60	$8.19	$9.14	$12.10	$7.55		$46.50	$142.08
TUES	Convention				$58.60		$6.44	$23.12	$3.18			$91.34
WED	Theirtown	Yourtown	229			$4.78	$6.55					$11.33
THURS												
FRI												
	TOTALS		458		175.80	12.97	30.03	46.62	14.88			$326.80

*** EXPLANATION**

MISC. June 16: Purchased management training tape at convention

ELAPSED BUSINESS MILES/KILOMETERS

Previous Total	
Current Week	458
Total to Date	458
CREDIT CARD BILLS	

Bus. MI/KM   458 @ 0.2 = $91.60

TOTAL EXPENSE	$418.40
Less Advance	$400.00
Balance	$18.40

☐ Claimed   ☐ Refunded

Signature of Claimant:

Approved by:

Date:

Figure 8.1: Sample expense report.

Keeping an Eye on the Future

As your consulting service grows, there are many new elements to your task of managing a successful business. You must consider and plan for the loss of a key person or the business structure. You must remind yourself to enjoy what you're doing. You must review your options if the business fails. You must consider the long term and begin planning for retirement. Planning well for tomorrow can reduce your worries today.

Succession in a Proprietorship

The personal skills, reputation, and management ability of the sole proprietor help to make the business successful. Without these human values the business is worth only the liquidation value of the tangible assets.

The sole proprietor's personal and business assets are one and the same. When a proprietor dies, the loss can become a financial disaster to the estate and the business. The business that was producing a good living for the owner and family will become a defunct business. What are the options?

The business may be transferred to a capable family member as a gift through provisions in the proprietor's will or by a sale provided through a prearranged purchase agreement effective at death. Cash is needed to offset losses to the business caused by the owner's death, to equalize the value of bequests made to other family members if the transfer is a gift, and to provide the sale price if the transfer is through sale.

If the buyer is a key employee, competitor, or third party, the business may be transferred at death, based on a prearranged sale agreement. However, cash is needed to provide a business continuation fund to meet expenses and perhaps to offset losses until the business adjusts to the new management.

If future management is not available then the business must be liquidated. Cash is needed to offset the difference between the business's going-concern value and its auction-block liquidation value, to provide a fund for income replacement to the family, and to pay outstanding business debts.

Succession in a Partnership

Unless there is a written agreement to the contrary, the death of a partner automatically dissolves the firm. In the absence of such an agreement, surviving partners have no right to buy the deceased's partnership interest. Surviving partners cannot assume the goodwill or take over the assets without consent of the deceased partner's estate. If the deceased was in debt to the partnership, the estate must settle the account in full and in cash.

The surviving partners act as liquidating trustees. They have exclusive possession of firm property but no right to carry on the business. If the business is continued, the surviving partners must share all profits with the deceased partner's estate and are liable for all losses. They must convert everything into cash at the best price obtainable. They must make an accounting to the deceased's estate and divide the proceeds with the estate. They must liquidate themselves out of their business and income.

What are the options a business has on the death of a partner?

If the surviving partner and deceased's heirs do nothing, the business is liquidated, resulting in auction price value for the salable assets. The business may receive nothing for goodwill. This is a disastrous solution for both the deceased partner's family and the surviving partners. It means termination of jobs for the surviving partners and employees.

The surviving partners may attempt to reorganize the partnership by taking the heirs into the partnership. But if heirs are unable to work in the business, the surviving partners must do all the work and share the profits. They could accept a new partner picked by the heirs. The surviving partners could also sell their interest in the business to the heirs, or conversely, buy out the heirs' interest.

Of course, there are some preparations that can be made prior to the death of a partner that will make a reorganization smoother. Buy and sell agreements funded with life insurance should be entered into while all partners are alive. Such an agreement, drafted by an attorney, will typically include a commitment by each partner not to dispose of his or her interest without first offering it at an agreed sale price to the partnership. The agreement will also include a provision for the partnership to buy a deceased partner's interest. The funding of the purchase will typically be from the proceeds of a life insurance policy written for that specific purpose.

Succession in a Corporation

The death of a stockholder who has been active in the operation of a closely held corporation allows the business entity to continue its legal structure, but not its personal structure. The interests of the heirs of the deceased inevitably come in conflict with the interests of the surviving associates.

What options are available to surviving stockholders?

The deceased's family may retain the stock interest. If the heirs have a majority interest, they may choose to become personally involved in management in order to receive income. Or they may choose to remain inactive, elect a new board of directors, and force the company to pay dividends. In either case, the surviving stockholders may lose a voice in management and possibly their jobs, while the deceased's family may become heirs to a business on the brink of failure. If the heirs have a minority interest and are not employed by the surviving associates, their only means of receiving an income from the corporation will be through dividends.

After the death of a stockholder, the deceased's heirs or estate may offer to sell the stock interest to the surviving stockholders. Or an outside buyer may be interested in purchasing stock in the corporation. While all of the interested parties are alive, they can enter into a binding buy and sell agreement funded with life insurance. This is done with a stockholder's buy and sell agreement drawn up with the assistance of your corporate attorney and accountant.

Succession in a Limited Liability Company

A limited liability company is similar in structure to a partnership. Therefore, partners should provide for the contingency of one another's death, incapacity, or desire to sell equity in the partnership agreement or in a buy and sell agreement. In the absence of such an agreement, surviving partners have no right nor obligation to buy the deceased's partnership interest. If the surviving partner and deceased's heirs do nothing, the business is liquidated, resulting in auction price value for the salable assets.

Buy and sell agreements should be entered into while all partners are alive. The agreement will include a commitment by each partner not to dispose of his or her interest without first offering it at an agreed sale price to the partnership. The agreement will also include a provision for the partnership to buy a deceased partner's interest. The purchase is usually funded from the proceeds of a life insurance policy written for that specific purpose.

Death of Key Employees

Many growing firms develop key employees who represent assets the firm cannot afford to be without. Even though these key employees may not own an interest in the firm, they are nonetheless valuable to its continuation. So what happens if a key employee dies?

Consulting services with key employees should consider life insurance payable to the firm on the death or disability of these people. How much life insurance? It should be an amount sufficient to offset financial losses during the readjustment period, to retain good credit standing, and to assure clients and suppliers that the company will continue as usual. In addition, key-employee insurance could retire loans, mortgages, bonds, attract and train a successor, or carry out ongoing plans for expansion and new developments. Talk to your insurance agent about the appropriate policy for insuring your business against the loss of a proprietor, a partner, a stockholder, or a key employee. It's one of the costs of growth.

Enjoying What You Do

John D. Rockefeller, who had both friends and businesses, once said, "A friendship founded on business is better than a business founded on friendship."

The primary reason you started your own business was to increase your opportunities to enjoy life. You wanted to offer a needed service, you wanted to help others, you wanted to extend your skills in your trade and in business, you wanted to be able to afford the better things of life. However, you didn't want to spend your entire waking time working. In fact, you may get so caught up in the chase for success that you miss the opportunities that success brings along the way.

Those who have found success in the consulting services and other fields will tell you that success is often empty if not shared with others. And that doesn't mean waiting until a successful destination—say at $1 million net worth—is reached. It means sharing success with others along the way, on a day-to-day basis. Maybe, for you, this means sharing your success with your family, a few good friends, or a charitable organization. In any case, consider that your financial success will mean much more to you if you can use it to bring physical, emotional, or spiritual success to others.

Manage your life outside your business as you do your time at the business. Look for ways of helping others. Find methods of giving yourself the things you most enjoy, whether time with friends, time with hobbies, time with competitive sports, time alone, or all of the above. Especially, take time to recharge your batteries. You will use lots of personal energy in starting, managing, and growing your consulting services business. Make sure you take the time to reenergize yourself.

When to Quit

The failure rate of new businesses is very high. It lowers as your consulting service matures. The longer you're in business, the greater the chance that you will continue in business. However, your consulting services business can fail at any time, quite often due to poor record keeping. So a key element of continued success is maintaining good records and learning how to manage by them.

But there may come a time when business conditions require that you throw in the towel. If you're not making sufficient profit or are reducing your capital to losses, you will soon be in financial trouble. What to do?

First, cut overhead as much as possible. The sooner this is done, the longer your business will survive—maybe long enough to find a solution.

Next, sell unused or inefficient assets. Of course, you must maintain your working tools. But maybe you can move your office to a less expensive location—even back home.

Then talk with your creditors about the situation and what you plan to do. Some may be very helpful in offering a workable solution—an extension of credit, assistance in finding additional contracts, or even purchase of stock in your business.

Finally, as necessary, talk with your attorney about your legal obligations and options. No one wants to declare bankruptcy, but it may be necessary. Or you may decide to set up a payment schedule for all debts and return to the work force as an employee.

There is no shame in failing to succeed, just in failing to try. If there are things you've learned from the experience, you can use them to increase your worth to an employer. Who better to manage a consulting services business than one who has learned what doesn't work.

Of course, now that you've planned out how to minimize losses, you probably won't have to. In fact, you can look forward to retirement.

Selling Your Consulting Business

A profitable consulting business is a valuable property that can be sold as you choose to retire or to move into another situation. How much can you get for your business? Of course, much depends on how successful your business is. Once established and showing a profit for three years or more, a consulting service will typically be valued at the replacement cost of tangible assets plus 0.75 to 1.25 times gross annual billing.

For example, a successful consulting service billing $500,000 a year from an office valued at $25,000 will typically sell for $400,000 (500,000 × 0.75 + 25,000) to $650,000 (500,000 × 1.25 + 25,000). Quite a range. As it probably took you 9 to 18 months to build your consulting business to a point of profitability, the price should repay you for this lost income as well as the physical assets the business has acquired. How much above or below this guideline you get depends on the value of your businesses name in gaining new clients. If your consulting business is on the threshhold of expansion, you will get more in the sale than if it is just paying its bills.

You can fund your retirement or future activities by selling your business on a contract. Depending on the buyer, you may want 25 percent down and the balance paid over five to ten years. Or you may opt to take a smaller purchase price and require an annual royalty on gross billings or on net profits. Once your consulting business gets to this point, you'll have a better idea of what you want and how you want it.

Planning to Retire

When should you retire from your profitable consulting services business? When you want to. Some consultants will hold off retiring until they are no longer physically able to work their trade. Others make plans to retire when they are 65 or even 62 years of age. Still others give their business 10 or 20 years to grow, then sell it to semiretire or move to a different trade. Some work their children into it, then gradually turn it over to them.

Some successful consulting services business owners will sell their shares to a partner or to another corporation. Others will sell or give their equity in the business to a relative. Some will sell out to key employees or to competitors.

The business can be sold outright for cash, earning the owner a cash settlement for his equity; or the seller can carry the paper or sell it on a contract with a downpayment and monthly payments for a specified term. In this case, buyers will often require the seller to sign a noncompetition contract that says the seller can't go to work for a competing consulting service or start another consulting services business in the same market.

Action Guidelines

This is the end of the beginning. You now have many of the tools you need to start and succeed with your own consulting service. Here's how you can put this final chapter into action:

✔ Apply the problem-solving techniques in this chapter to a current problem that your consulting service is facing or expects to face.

✔ Even if you don't plan to hire anyone, review the methods of managing employees. If nothing else, it will remind you of why you don't want to increase your staff for awhile.

✔ If you have or expect to hire employees, review the information on benefits programs to determine which best fit your business and philosophy.

✔ Find a local temporary employment office who may be able to help you during busy times.

✔ Consult with your insurance agent to make sure you are not undercovered or overbilled.

✔ Plan today for how your business will survive the death of a principal, partner, or key employee.

✔ Periodically review your expenses to ensure you are getting the most from each dollar you spend.

✔ Have fun with your consulting service and your life!

RESOURCES
FOR SMALL BUSINESS

These publications on proven management techniques for small businesses are available from Upstart Publishing Company, Inc., 155 North Wacker Drive, Chicago, IL 60606. For a free current catalog of small business books and resources, call (800) 829-7934 or (312) 836-4400, ext. 650 in Illinois.

The Business Planning Guide, 6th edition, 1992, David H. Bangs, Jr. and Upstart Publishing Company, Inc. A manual that helps you write a business plan and financing proposal tailored to your business, your goals, and your resources. Includes worksheets and checklists. (Softcover, 208 pp., $19.95)

The Market Planning Guide, 4th edition, 1994, David H. Bangs, Jr. and Upstart Publishing Company, Inc. A manual to help small-business owners put together a goal-oriented, resource-based marketing plan with action steps, benchmarks and time lines. Includes worksheets and checklists to make implementation and review easier. (Softcover, 180 pp., $19.95)

The Cash Flow Control Guide, 1990, David H. Bangs, Jr. and Upstart Publishing Company, Inc. A manual to help small-business owners solve their number one financial problem. Includes worksheets and checklists. (Softcover, 88 pp., $14.95)

The Personnel Planning Guide, 1988, David H. Bangs, Jr. and Upstart Publishing Company, Inc. A 176-page manual outlining practical, proven personnel management techniques, including hiring, managing, evaluating and compensating personnel. Includes worksheets and checklists. (Softcover, 176 pp., $19.95)

The Start Up Guide: A One-Year Plan for Entrepreneurs, 2nd edition, 1994, David H. Bangs, Jr. and Upstart Publishing Company, Inc. This book utilizes the same step-by-step, no-jargon method as *The Business Planning Guide,* to help even those with no business training through the process of beginning a successful business. (Softcover, 176 pp., $19.95)

Managing By the Numbers: Financial Essentials for the Growing Business, 1992, David H. Bangs, Jr. and Upstart Publishing Company, Inc. Straightforward techniques for getting the maximum return with a minimum of detail in your business's financial management. (Softcover, 160 pp., $19.95)

Building Wealth, 1992, David H. Bangs, Jr. and the editors of *Common Sense.* A collection of tested techniques designed to help you plan your personal finances and how to plan your business finances to benefit you, your family, and employees. (Softcover, 168 pp., $19.95)

Buy the Right Business—At the Right Price, 1990, Brian Knight and the Associates of Country Business, Inc. Many people who would like to be in business for themselves think strictly of starting a business. In some cases, buying a going concern may be preferable—and just as affordable. (Softcover, 152 pp., $18.95)

Borrowing for Your Business, 1991, George M. Dawson. This is a book for borrowers and about lenders. Includes detailed guidelines on how to select a bank and a banker, how to answer the lender's seven most important questions, how your banker looks at a loan, and how to get a loan renewed. (Hardcover, 160 pp., $19.95)

Can This Partnership Be Saved? 1992, Peter Wylie and Mardy Grothe. The authors offer solutions and hope for problems between key people in business. (Softcover, 272 pp., $19.95)

Cases in Small Business Management, 1994, John Edward de Young. A compilation of intriguing and useful case studies in typical small business problems. (Softcover, 258 pp., $24.95)

The Complete Guide to Selling Your Business, 1992, Paul Sperry and Beatrice Mitchell. A step-by-step guide through the entire process from how to determine when the time is right to sell to negotiating the final terms. (Hardcover, 160 pp., $21.95)

The Complete Selling System, 1991, Pete Frye. This book can help any manager or salesperson, even those with no experience, find the solutions to some of the most common dilemmas in managing sales. (Hardcover, 192 pp., $21.95)

Creating Customers, 1992, David H. Bangs, Jr. and the editors of *Common Sense.* A book for business owners and managers who want a step-by-step approach to selling and promoting. Techniques include inexpensive market research, pricing your goods and services and writing a usable marketing plan. (Softcover, 176 pp., $19.95)

The Entrepreneur's Guide to Going Public, 1994, James B. Arkebauer with Ron Schultz. A comprehensive and useful book on a subject that is the ultimate dream of most entrepreneurs—making an initial public offering (IPO). (Softcover, 368 pp., $19.95)

Export Profits, 1992, Jack S. Wolf. This book shows how to find the right foreign markets for your product, cut through the red tape, minimize currency risks, and find the experts who can help. (Softcover, 304 pp., $19.95)

Financial Troubleshooting, 1992, David H. Bangs, Jr. and the editors of *Common Sense.* This book helps the owner/manager use basic diagnostic methods to monitor the health of the business and solve problems before damage occurs. (Softcover, 192 pp., $19.95)

Financial Essentials for Small Business Success, 1994, Joseph Tabet and Jeffrey Slater. Designed to show readers where to get the information they need and how planning and recordkeeping will enhance the health of any small business. (Softcover, 272 pp., $19.95)

From Kitchen to Market, 1992, Stephen Hall. A practical approach to turning culinary skills into a profitable business. (Softcover, 208 pp., $24.95)

The Home-Based Entrepreneur, 1993, Linda Pinson and Jerry Jinnett. A step-by-step guide to all the issues surrounding starting a home-based business. Issues such as zoning, labor laws, and licensing are discussed and forms are provided to get you on your way. (Softcover, 192 pp., $19.95)

Keeping the Books, 1993, Linda Pinson and Jerry Jinnett. Basic business recordkeeping both explained and illustrated. Designed to give you a clear understanding of small business accounting by taking you step-by-step through general records, development of financial statements, tax reporting, scheduling, and financial statement analysis. (Softcover, 208 pp., $19.95)

The Language of Small Business, 1994, Carl O. Trautmann. A clear, concise dictionary of small business terms for students and small business owners. (Softcover, 416 pp., $19.95)

Marketing Your Invention, 1992, Thomas Mosley. This book dispels the myths and clearly communicates what inventors need to know to successfully bring their inventions to market. (Softcover, 232 pp., $19.95)

100 Best Retirement Businesses, 1994, Lisa Angowski Rogak with David H. Bangs, Jr. A one-of-a-kind book bringing retirees the inside information on the most interesting and most lucrative businesses for them. (Softcover, 416 pp., $15.95)

The Small Business Computer Book, 1993, Robert Moskowitz. This book does not recommend particular systems, but rather provides readers with a way to think about these choices and make the right decisions for their businesses. (Softcover, 190 pp., $19.95)

Start Your Own Business for $1,000 or Less, 1994, Will Davis. Shows readers how to get started in the "mini-business" of their dreams with less than $1,000. (Softcover, 280 pp., $17.95)

Steps to Small Business Start-Up, 1993, Linda Pinson and Jerry Jinnett. A step-by-step guide for starting and succeeding with a small or home-based business. Takes you through the mechanics of business startup and gives an overview of information on such topics as copyrights, trademarks, legal structures, recordkeeping, and marketing. (Softcover, 256 pp., $19.95)

Target Marketing for the Small Business, 1993, Linda Pinson and Jerry Jinnett. A comprehensive guide to marketing your business. This book not only shows you how to reach your customers, it also gives you a wealth of information on how to research that market through the use of library resources, questionnaires, demographics, etc. (Softcover, 176 pp., $19.95)

On Your Own: A Woman's Guide to Starting Your Own Business, 2nd edition, 1993, Laurie Zuckerman. *On Your Own is* for women who want hands-on, practical information about starting and running their own business. It deals honestly with issues like finding time for your business when you're also the primary care provider, societal biases against women and credit discrimination. (Softcover, 320 pp., $19.95)

Problem Employees, 1991, Dr. Peter Wylie and Dr. Mardy Grothe. Provides managers and supervisors with a simple, practical and straightforward approach to help all employees, especially problem employees, significantly improve their work performance. (Softcover, 272 pp., $22.95)

Problems and Solutions in Small Business Management, 1994, the editors of *Forum,* the journal of the Association of Small Business Development Centers. A collection of case studies selected from the pages of *Forum* magazine. (Softcover, 200 pp., $21.95)

The Restaurant Planning Guide, 1992, Peter Rainsford and David H. Bangs, Jr. This book takes the practical techniques of *The Business Planning Guide* and combines it with the expertise of Peter Rainsford, a restaurateur and a professor at the Cornell School of Hotel Administration. Topics include: establishing menu prices, staffing and scheduling, controlling costs and niche marketing. (Softcover, 176 pp., $19.95)

Successful Retailing, 2nd edition, 1993, Paula Wardell. Provides hands-on help for those who want to start or expand their retail business. Sections include: strategic planning, marketing and market research and inventory control. (Softcover, 176 pp., $19.95)

The Upstart Guide to Owning and Managing an Antiques Business, 1994, Lisa Angowski Rogak. Provides the information a prospective antiques dealer needs to run a business profitably. (Softcover, 224 pp., $15.95)

The Upstart Guide to Owning and Managing a Bar or Tavern, 1994, Roy Alonzo. Provides essential information on planning, making the initial investment, financial management, and marketing a bar or tavern. (Softcover, 256 pp., $15.95)

The Upstart Guide to Owning and Managing a Bed & Breakfast, 1995, Lisa Angowski Rogak. Provides information on choosing the best location, licensing and what really goes on behind the scenes. (Softcover, 224 pp., $15.95)

The Upstart Guide to Owning and Managing a Desktop Publishing Service, 1995, Dan Ramsey. Explains how anyone with a flair for words, a sense of graphic design, and a willingness to buy a good computer can start a desktop publishing business. (Softcover, 201 pp., $15.95)

The Upstart Guide to Owning and Managing a Florist Service, 1995, Dan Ramsey. Provides information on starting up a full-service florist business, including information on location, setup of the actual flower shop, and lists of resources and suppliers. (Softcover, 224 pp., $ 15.95)

The Upstart Guide to Owning and Managing a Résumé Service, 1995, Dan Ramsey. Shows how any reader can turn personnel, writing, and computer skills into a lucrative résumé-writing business. (Softcover, 224 pp., $15.95)

The Upstart Guide to Owning and Managing a Newsletter Business, 1995, Lisa Angowski Rogak. All the reader needs to begin a newsletter business, including topics, how to do a market analysis, what equipment to buy, and daily operations information. Extensive resources and a business plan, too. (Softcover, 224 pp., $15.95)

The Upstart Guide to Owning and Managing a Travel Service, 1995, Dan Ramsey. Provides detailed information on becoming a business owner and self-employed travel agent—either consumer or business travel, or both—including advice on necessary equipment, location, and marketing. (Softcover, 224 pp., $15.95)

The Woman Entrepreneur, 1992, Linda Pinson and Jerry Jinnett. Thirty-three successful women business owners share their practical ideas for success and their sources for inspiration. (Softcover, 244 pp., $14.00)

Other Available Titles

The Complete Guide to Business Agreements, 1993, Ted Nicholas, Enterprise • Dearborn. Contains 127 of the most commonly needed business agreements. (Loose-leaf binder, $69.95)

The Complete Small Business Legal Guide, 1993, Robert Friedman, Enterprise • Dearborn. Provides the hands-on help you need to start a business, maintain all necessary records, properly hire and fire employees, and deal with the many changes a business goes through. (Loose-leaf binder, $69.95)

Guerrilla Marketing: Secrets for Making Big Profits from Your Small Business, 1984, J. Conrad Levinson, Houghton-Mifflin. A classic tool kit for small businesses. (Hardcover, 226 pp., $14.95)

How to Form Your Own Corporation Without a Lawyer for Under $75.00, 1992, Ted Nicholas, Enterprise • Dearborn. A good book for helping you to discover all the unique advantages of incorporating while at the same time learning how quick, easy, and inexpensive the process can be. (Softcover, $19.95)

Marketing Sourcebook for Small Business, 1989, Jeffrey P. Davidson, John Wylie Publishing. A good introductory book for small business owners with excellent definitions of important marketing terms and concepts. (Hardcover, 325 pp., $24.95)

The Small Business Survival Kit: 101 Troubleshooting Tips for Success, 1993, John Ventura, Enterprise • Dearborn. Offers compassionate insight into the emotional side of financial difficulties as well as a nuts-and-bolts consideration of options for the small businessperson experiencing tough times. (Softcover, $19.95)

INDEX

209

Slogan, 66
Small Business Administration (SBA), 113; guaranteed loans, 152-153; On-Line service, 58; resources, 57-59; Small Business Answer Desk, 57
Small Business Institutes, 59
Social Security Act of 1935, 72
Social security insurance (FICA), 100, 113, 169
Software. *See individual manufacturers*
Sole proprietorship, 74-75, 190-191
Spread, 151
Spreadsheets, 31
Standard industrial classification (SIC), 67
Standard Metropolitan Statistical Areas (SMSAs), 122
Start-up. *See also specific aspects of;* action guidelines, 85; business location and, 67-72; business plan for, 63-65; costs, 40-42; employment laws and, 72-73
State employment services, 111
Statement of purpose, 64-65
Stationery, 187-188
Stock, 78-79
Stockholder, death of, 192-193
Stress; time and, 45; tolerance, 24
Sub-Chapter S corporations, 59, 80, 113
Success, business plan and, 63-65
Succession; corporation, 192-193; limited liability company, 193; partnership, 191-192; proprietorship, 190-191
Supplies/materials, 10, 16, 38-39

T
Tax collection agent, 113
Taxes; accountant and, 83; corporations and, 79-80; information resources, 59-61; partnerships and, 77; proprietorships and, 74; records for, 91, 93; understanding and paying, 113-114
Tax payable report, 138
Telephone, 16; long-distance calls, 188; services, 37; yellow pages advertising, 130-131
Television, 128, 129
Temporary help, 188
Temporary personnel services, 174-175
Time; management, 43-48; stress and, 45

Time management planning systems, 44-48
Tools, 12-13, 26
Total costs, 89
Trade associations, 13, 53-54
Trade Journals, 55
Travel expenses, 188
Travel time, 43

U
Unemployment compensation insurance (FUTA), 169
Uniform Partnership Act (UPA), 75
United States Census Bureau, 122
United States Department of Commerce; Office of Business Liaison, 122; Small Business Administration. *See* Small Business Administration (SBA)
Unqualified retirement plans, 171

V
Value(s); personal, 23-25; *vs.* price, 105-107
Variable costs, 89
Variable expenses, 186
Variable rate interest, 151

W
W-2 form, 100
W-4 form, 101
Windows, 30, 31
Wonderlic Personnel Tests, 112
WordPerfect, 31
Word processors, 31
WordStar, 31
Workers' compensation insurance, 169
Workers' compensation insurance, 179, 181
Working capital, 157-158
Work schedule, 43

X
XyWrite, 31

Y
Yellow pages advertising, 130-131

Z
Zoning laws, 71-72